THE NAKED PILOT

THE NAKED PILOT

How a Scotsman Crashed a Messerschmitt on North Weald

JAMES HARDIE

authorHOUSE®

AuthorHouse™ UK
1663 Liberty Drive
Bloomington, IN 47403 USA
www.authorhouse.co.uk
Phone: 0800.197.4150

Published by AuthorHouse 03/19/2015

ISBN: 978-1-5049-3940-9 (sc)
ISBN: 978-1-5049-3941-6 (e)

Print information available on the last page.

This book is printed on acid-free paper.

Contents

Introduction

This is a hands-on, imagination-on story of an aeroplane. It details the process of learning to fly and committing to take off, climbing, and cruising. It also discusses managing a sixty-two-year-old, rebuilt, French/German Nord 1101 (the only one flying in Britain today). Brought into the story is an equally old motorcycle rebuilt at the same time, which lights the imagination on fire.

I am particularly interested in what I call the *naked pilots*. These pilots are spiritual successors to Cervantes's character, Don Quixote, a man whose imagination helps him deal with the impossible and connect the mysterious extravagance of innocence to life-and-death situations.

My naked pilots are Bill Burns (1921–1972), Amy Johnson (1903–1941), and Antoine de Saint-Exupéry (1900–1944). I knew Bill Burns personally and worked beside him in Aberdeen College of Education from 1968 to 1971. He started flying before the Second World War and was called up to the RAF just as he was sitting his B license for commercial flying. He had a serious crash and was taken out of the RAF in 1942 as a result. His rehabilitation program gave him the choice to knit, crochet, or paint, and after choosing painting, he went to the Glasgow School of Art (1944–1948).

A variety of books and films about Amy Johnson's short life have been produced. She became a public figure and raised the hopes and dreams of thousands in the 1930's. She was only thirty seven when she disappeared over the Thames Estuary in January 1941. I had an art exhibition in Glasgow in 1993 called *Naked Pilot,* in which I tried to explore the many faces of Amy in paintings and prints. I then realised that I wanted a stronger connection to flight.

The most famous of the naked pilots is Antoine de Saint-Exupéry. He was a pilot and writer, and his books are still among the most read in France. His disappearance has been visited and revisited by many French citizens. *The Little Prince* is likely one of the most famous titles in the world, despite being written roughly seventy years ago.

To me, these three naked pilots were great artists of the twentieth century. The different ways they lived and their sublime connection to flying must be considered art.

The whole adventure started for me one wet night in October 1958. I had emerged from Hamilton West Station carrying a heavy portfolio from Glasgow School of Art. I stood at the deserted bus stop, and my imagination felt as bedraggled and frustrated as the rest of me. The timetable read, "No buses after 6:00 p.m." It was 6:15.

As I looked around, I saw that lights were still on in Ross Motors across the street. I knew the branch in Glasgow sold motorcycles and wondered whether I could find a motorcycle with a sidecar to transport my portfolio. I staggered across the street and found the salesman just about to close his shop. He happened to have an old, cheap motorcycle, but he warned me that it was a bit peculiar.

At the back of the shop stood a long, low bike with a flat, wide tank and girder forks. He said, "It's some kind of Brough that was just exchanged for a car. The owner drove it here, so I know it still works." I had never seen the Rolls Royce of motorcycles, the Brough Superior. It was famous because of its connection to Lawrence of Arabia (he owned seven), but I felt my imagination had been sparked.

Ultimately, the car salesman apologised for the motorcycle's old-fashioned, rusty appearance, and he gratefully accepted my twenty-five pounds.

BBC Radio in New York, Glasgow, and Aberdeen

My daughter, Gwen Hardie, and I are about to record an interview for BBC Radio Scotland's "A Chip off the Old Block." Gwen is in a New York Studio, I'm in a BBC Scotland Studio in Glasgow, and our interviewer, Mark Stephen, is located in BBC Aberdeen.

Altogether, there will be four sets of interviews with fathers and sons or fathers and daughters. Gwen and I are the third pairing. I switch on the radio to hear the very first programme at 6:00 a.m. on 5 May 2009 (Saturday). It's very early in the morning to listen to such probing questions and engaging answers, but there's no sign of strain as the parent talks about his life as a church minister and the son speaks about following in his father's footsteps. And then we hear the key statement: "I always wanted to be myself" from the son. His father's journeys, especially abroad, opened doors for him into politics and religion that were not so different from a life filled with art. In our recording, to be transmitted on 19 May 2009, I wonder whether I've been too quick with my answers to provocative questions, too quick to tell stories. Art does this to you – so does flying. Gwen and I should have talked more gently.

Tarkovsky, the filmmaker, believed that a poetic logic might be closer to our lived experience – internal rather than external. Storytelling, by contrast, is melodramatic and full of tricks and artifice. When we talk on the radio, it is so easy to let our stories take over and ride roughshod over more important connections. Flight testing an aeroplane solo brings together connections on all sorts of levels. After a break from flying, both the pilot and the aeroplane have to build up a working relationship again. There is another type of radio in the cockpit of the aeroplane that connects to the air traffic controllers. The pilot repeats all the directions back to the controller and is supposed to control the flying machine, especially in regards to take off and landing.

I see that the altimeter has water or something in the pipe this May morning, which means it's difficult to determine my height. It shows us well below ground or well above it when all we're trying to do is set the barometric pressure while on the ground at Prestwick Airport. The plane's radio has the same wantonness, probably as a result of some water somewhere. I know that the sun and dry wind do more for old aeroplanes than tinkering about though, and after three flights Golf Bravo Sierra Mike Delta begins to get back to being her old self.

The undercarriage works well and the hydraulic pressure is high. I figure it's probably only air blocks causing our troubles, and those are purged now. All this work on an aeroplane costs real money. I shudder a bit as I remember the money problems most pilots face. One of the naked pilot's stands out, Antoine de Saint-Exupéry. This famous French pilot and writer decided to go for a large cash prize in 1935, just a few days before the end of the year (when the prize would be withdrawn). The prize was offered for the first flight from Paris to Saigon. The amazing story of his crash in Egypt with his mechanic, Prevot, showed he had set out with two coffee flasks and half a bottle of wine. He didn't win any money, but his rescue and the story that came out of it eventually brought him great wealth.

Saint-Exupéry's Caudron Simoun had a Renault 240 hp engine with an adjustable Ratier propeller similar to my own Nord 1101. When his Simoun crashed on a high plateau, the water and fuel tanks shattered. Saint-Exupéry and Prevot were left with just the coffee and the wine for survival. Stranded and lost in the desert, they decided to walk north until they collapsed. That was how a French pilot, Guillaumet, a great friend of Saint-Exupéry's, tried to save himself in the Andes, and Saint-Exupéry and Prevot decided to follow his example. Luckily, they were found by two Bedouins before they perished. What a story!

And yet Saint-Exupéry was surrounded by the most professional aviators in the whole of France. At that time, Aeropostale was leading the world of aviation. Daurat, the head of Aeropostale, the man who sent pilots to deliver mail in all sorts of weather had Saint-Exupéry's Caudron Simoun fitted out specifically for long-distance flying. The maps were drawn up by professional navigators. Plus, the Simoun had flown thousands of miles without a hint of trouble; in fact, everything had been done to ensure that Saint-Exupéry would win the big prize. But a naked pilot is a naked pilot.

When Saint-Exupéry returned to Paris after a month of recuperation, he was met with a hero's welcome. But he owed so much money that he was afraid of his landlady! He had to persuade a friend to go with him to make peace with the formidable woman so he could retrieve his gold watch and small dog!

Long after those amazing moments, I move my camcorder onto the copilot's seat. *Can I fly the plane and operate the bullet camera at the same time?* I wonder. The camera is mounted on the floor of the plane, and the leads are long enough for me to select play and start it up. I then move the joystick and select execute to begin recording. I see the grey, concrete runway on the screen of the camcorder and start up the aeroplane.

I know I need to connect to Deepsykehead Farm and use the amazing morning light for recording. It's like the BBC programme, but it's happening in the air.

* * *

New York, Glasgow, Aberdeen. The voices come from across the world without any hesitation; it's as though we were sitting right beside each other. Later, the programme is edited and we have lift-off. My voice sounds slightly cracked and old, but as Gwen's voice uncoils, it sounds sure and steady. Mark Stephen, the interviewer, says, "You can tell us, Jim, because no one is listening, obviously."

How odd it is to be born and live a life. It all seems so casual and improbable. A child has a little mouth and eyes, and what does the parent put in front of the child? As a parent, all I remember is the "first-time" syndrome: my first time becoming a parent, my first time creating a family, my first time earning a living. Everything is taken for granted. The child sees none of this. The happenings slowly open up a perspective of family life. Places become very important – they become spaces to be filled by a growing human being. The Old Schoolhouse at Fetternear in Aberdeenshire have become a focus for the Hardie family. Gwen gives her perspective on life there for children aged 8–18.

How do you define yourself as an artist, Gwen? How do you define yourself as an artist, Jim? I hear myself saying things that I have hardly thought about for years. Like one of my old art teachers, Jim Barclay, told me once, that I needed to avoid being crafty and embrace being natural and practical while trying to develop. I passed this advice to Gwen, but she was different and felt inspired by simple things. Also, she sought an existential connection in her painting. She was rather isolated as a small child in Fetternear, and her bedroom seemed too large and frightening to her, but it gave her the space to follow her inner world completely. The questions flow and the answers are unveiled. I explain that I am a Taurean and have read that Taureans are keen on helping people be independent and find their own way, to find the courage to pursue what they believe in. Gwen surprised me by saying, "Dad named me Gwen after Gwen John." I remembered trying to think of names that couldn't be shortened such as James to Jim, Mary to Minnie, or Elizabeth to Betty, and I thought that Amy and Gwen couldn't get much shorter. But my daughters have a mysterious connection to Gwen John and Amy Johnson. Gwen found this fascinating, and for years, she was inspired by Gwen John's penetrating study of ordinary things (even though her painting is very different in style). She said, "Gwen John's paintings, on the surface, are very different to mine – very different technique and style. But this gentle but deep look at the internal as seen on the surface [makes me] feel a psychological connection to my namesake."

Family File Storytellers

I was guided through the world of mystery, the space between the divine and the chaotic, by my family's storytellers. Stories reveal a great deal about the tellers, and in the west of Scotland, where not much is acknowledged as it is happening, stories can provide an insight into the dreams and anguish of family life. In large families, one has to listen and grasp the bigger picture quickly, especially at family meals. When there are ten of you around the table, one must concentrate. My mother, Mary Stirrat Morton, was our family's main storyteller. She was also the purveyor of food. She crafted stories to suit the different personalities in the family. In later years, as Mary Morton Hardie, she wrote her stories down in an amazing book, *A Cinder Glows,* which was published in 1989, and again in 1993.

Mary Morton Hardie

In 1916, Mary's father, George Morton of Motherwell, was reported missing in France during the battle of Arras in the First World War. Mum had three sisters: Ella, Gertie, and Gina. What follows is from Mother's book, *A Cinders Glows -The Telegram.*[8]

"When Mama saw Kirsty, she gave a hoarse cry and burst into tears, sobbing so deeply and painfully that Gina and I cried too. Kirsty laid her baby on the thick ragrug in front of the fire then enveloped Mama in her arms with many 'Dear mothers of God' and 'Holy Marys.' Other women neighbours slipped in, asking 'What news'? They sensed it was bad. Often telegrams were sent to wives to let them know their men were coming home on leave. Then everyone laughed and joked but not this time. Expectantly they crowded round. Kirsty lifted the yellow paper telegram and read out in her rich Irish voice these words; 'We regret to inform you that Sergeant George Morton has been reported missing, believed killed in Arras, France on or about 20th. Feb. 1916. Further information will be forwarded by letter'.

"Years passed and no further word was heard from Sergeant George Morton. Some 3 years later on the 18th. Jan 1919, the same neighbour Kirsty banged on the Morton's door in Motherwell. 'Look at the Paper!' the headlines stated that another hospital ship had docked at Southampton. The soldier's names were in long columns in alphabetical order. She ran her finger down, stopped, and then read out in a hoarse voice. 'Morton, George, Sergeant of the 1st. Battalion Royal Scots Regiment.'

"Mama and the children were aghast. They now had a boarder in their cottage called Hughie, a gentle quiet sort of a man who had got very friendly with their Mother and as the sisters put it they were getting ready for another sister. 'Mama stared at him, and then slipped sideways in her chair, half fainting. Hughie gave her a little water and when she spoke she whispered, 'What shall we do?' over and over again' Mum's story then went through a horrendous divorce after the returning war hero claimed custody of his four daughters, all under 12 years old. George had been badly wounded at Arras, as had been told to his family thrown into a cart as a dead man among the other dead men. The Germans had noticed he was still alive, though missing fingers, a shoulder and other body parts. The Scottish soldiers had been briefed to take an old farmhouse, only to be confronted by a 'bomber' battalion 'mortar' defence. The mortar shells had been deadly in no man's land and the whole company of Scottish Riflemen were thought to be killed The wounded George Morton was sent east to Prussia, where he recovered and was eventually able to come home."

My mother's main drama came after her father was rehabilitated. She and her sisters were sent to an orphanage at Queensferry in Fife and kept away from their mother, who had left for Ireland to start a new life with Hughie. In London, George met Beatrice, an American cancan dancer and decided to marry her, confident that he could produce sons instead of what he called useless daughters. But their alcoholic stepmother's abuse resulted in tragic consequences for the vulnerable children. We managed to persuade Mother to tell her story in a book, when she was in her eighties.

James Watterson Hardie

My father's defining feature was his blonde hair. He was a real Brylcreem boy. He was called up in 1941 and went into the RAF. He had sold his beloved motorbike and sidecar, and he bought an Austin 7 car just before he was called up. This little car remained on chocks in the garage for most of the war.

James Watterson Hardie

He was a careful man who took a kind of sensory satisfaction in caring for machinery. Even televisions had a dust sheet pinned over them at night. He always had a lit cigarette, and the smoke from it and his golden hair left an indelible impression on me. My father applied for aircrew, even joining the Royal Air Force Volunteer Reserve (RAFVR) to try to become a flight mechanic, but his eyesight and his age (older than 30) were against him. He became an airfield controller, though, which suited his style. There is a wonderful photograph of him on duty in his caravan with a Verey pistol and signalling lamps. His RAF pushbike remained with the family for a few years after the war. There was an interesting contrast between my father's stories and my mother's wonderful melodramas.

Mary Ann Watterson Hardie

Granny Hardie lived in Airbles Road in Motherwell for many years. There, she brought up her two sons, Tom and James – the latter was my father. Her husband, Andrew Hardie, died in 1938, and she moved from Motherwell to Fife. A native Fifer herself, she brought with her to Larkhall a whiff of salt air when she came back to live with us on and off until 1956. In our busy household, at the height, there were ten of us under one roof.

Granny's stories were exciting and unbelievable because we had no context for ships and the sea, the Battle of Trafalgar, or the Boer War. Her father was a sail maker who had sailed round the world and been shipwrecked three times. It wasn't until I moved to Fife in 1960 that Granny's stories became real to me. I became a painter, and the dreams and anguish of her stories and my chosen way of life chimed together as I painted Fife Ness in my studio at Lundin Links. Granny's most unbelievable stories were about Admiral Black, and her stylish grandmother was Admiral Black's sister. Captain Black really existed and left his house, Marsfield in Anstruther, to John Watterston, master mariner and Granny's grandfather. I got the details of the sea stories at the Royal Naval Museum, Portsmouth. Daring Jimmy Black, my granny's relative, was a Hornblower figure who had an amazing career in the Napoleonic Wars. He was most famous for cutting out rich prizes against the odds. In 1812, he was captain of a twenty-eight gun sloop, Weasel, and he fought to disrupt Napoleon's lines of supply in the Adriatic. Jimmy was shot through the hand, but he ignored the injury to concentrate on the fight. It was said that anybody could get into a fight, but it took a Jimmy Black to get himself and his crew out victoriously. He fought for twelve hours. The Weasel was a wreck, and the crew members were shattered – five people died and twenty-five were wounded, including Jimmy Black. The Weasel's people had to bring off French anchors to warp their ship out of the Bay of Bastoglina in Dalmatia. This was done slowly and laboriously because her people were half dead with fatigue and under fire from ashore and attacked by French gunboats. Still, Jimmy escaped successfully.

Granny Hardie told some of these life-and-death dramas in the accent of her grandmother, Janet Black, whose brother was the famous captain. Granny took on a posher, more English accent to account for the style and feistiness of the generation that had fought Napoleon. Before the cinema, radio, and TV, stories passed down to future generations concentrated on art, adventure, and love.

Rebuilding the Motorcycle and the Aeroplane

Our first family holiday after the war was to the Isle of Man for 1947 TT (Tourist Trophy) Week. When I was there, I felt like I was in the middle of the story at last. TT Week during the first week in June was much anticipated and much supported by the motorcycling fraternity. These were the first races to be held after the war, bringing together the best motorcycles and riders from around the world, and it was my first experience with the motorcycle in all its mystery. Many of the riders were returning servicemen, relieved to be alive and able to smell the wonderful Castrol R, a castor oil–based machine oil, which had the most incredible aroma when heated. The racetrack went round the island, through town streets, along country lanes, and even over a mountain. Landmarks included Governor's Bridge and Glencrutchery Road. I wondered, *Could the riders lap at an average speed of 100 mph?*

The race spectators, like my dad, wore their armed forces ties and scarves. Nobody mentioned the struggle that had ended two years before. They wandered quietly, expressing no emotion, no enthusiasm round the pits, round the small garages, old shops, barns, and byres where their glittering racing bikes stood. The bikes were in every position but upright. They were hoisted, propped, over on their side – wheels, cylinder heads, pistons, sprockets, chains, tyres, and other parts were missing. But there was always the sweet castor oil smell of warm Castrol R. The motorcycle companies such as B.S.A. and Velocette were just starting up. They had probably been making Spitfire parts during the war years. People seemed friendly to my 9-year-old eyes and nobody sent me away. I felt like I was part of the show. I absorbed through sight, smell, and taste. It was different but familiar. The Isle of Man was halfway between Ireland and Scotland, and people didn't shout like in England.

Bob Foster, Freddie Frith, Harold Daniel, and Artie Bell may well have been the most famous racers in the world, but they were also extremely self-effacing and kept up a gentle repartee with young and old. Crowds three and four deep gathered outside the pubs to watch them, and the good Isle of Man beer was passed around like spare motorcycle parts. Everybody seemed equal.

* * *

It's 2008. I'm 70 years old and talking to a motorcycle. The bike is sixty years old and looks it. The paint's a snazzy two-tone: cream and cerulean blue. The paint came from small aerosol cans. The colours looked good at the time, but I was impatient and only smoothed the strange metal sheet body of its contagion of rust. Now there's a funny, sugar-like texture pushing up under the shining paint. The bike last ran properly in the early 1980s, when its automatic advance and retard stuck in retard as though its life was one long tick over with no power left for zooming down the road. Oil oozed out onto the floor every time the bike was rested. The flywheel oil seal had faltered.

There's still a dialogue. The bike's the dream of the famous Goodman brothers who ran the Velocette firm of Hall Green Birmingham. I take the advance and retard over to the bench in my studio and rest it among paintings and paintbrushes and things that fall over with a bang and a clatter. The inner brass pins are supposed to slot into the cam plate and allow about a quarter of movement. Centrifugal force should be enough to move the cam so that the bulgy bit opens the points and a spark shoots off into the cylinder and explodes. But it sticks on the curve because it's retarded. I find a set of six tiny files, all about four inches long. They are round, flat, round and flat, square, and round and square. I use them to work gently at the parts. The metal hardly seems to change, but there is a glitter of particles underneath. *Am I missing something? Is the geometry so particular that it has long since been worn and distorted and unworkable? Am I making it worse?* I mix the various bits and pieces and say, "Eureka!" There's a silky movement. The part even springs back like it should. The high-tension spark comes from a very early BTH generator, and the bike is an early model. The Velocette Owners Club recommend I change to a Miller generator, which is much simpler and works better. The bike is a 200 cc LE Velocette and very difficult to work on, but I kneel on the floor and work away. I fill the bike with oil and water and try to start it. Water pours out of the cylinder heads and petrol pours out of the petrol tap. Everything has dried up and shrunk, and the water has frozen and cracked the engine (the alloy cylinders especially).

Back to the drawing board to try again. This time I put on my period helmet and ex-RAF goggles. The bike starts with difficulty, and then it's out of the garage and off down the road. It runs well for about 100 yards, and then it comes to a halt. I figure that it must be the advance and retard. I push the bike, and it starts again. The test is to get round the crescent twice. It starts then stops then starts then stops again, and I push it back to the house.

The next day, I notice that I have forgotten to turn off the fuel. I go through the starting procedure, and to my surprise, the engine fires up immediately. It still starts and stops, but I consider that may have something to do with the fuel flow. I must have used too much gasket goo on the taps and nearly blocked off the tiny orifices. I carefully take the side plate off the carburettor and check the fuel flow – there's hardly anything. With awkward freezing, and stiffening fingers, I scrape off the goo and try again, propping the bike on its side to get better access. I'm nearly finished when the bike topples over and the insides of the carburettor roll across the garage floor. I find the tiny float, but there's no more float needle. So it's back to the phone and the computer. I know there's probably only one place in the whole of Britain that stocks Amal parts.

Naked Pilot exhibition, Collins Gallery Glasgow, 1993

First Flight in Nord 1101

I'm still standing in my garage at my house in Skelmorlie on the Clyde coast. The back wall has a five-foot, circular hole through which the tail of my aeroplane stuck out into the damp Ayrshire air for nearly fourteen years. The fuselage and tail were suspended and propped up so that we could fit a new main spar from wing root to wing root (about nine foot long in all). There's also a small, irregular cut out in the side wall of the garage where we threaded the old, main spar out and the new one in. The wood of the garage has taken on a patina that makes it look as though it has always been like this, but I remember, back in 1993, when we wheeled the 1947 Nord 1101 onto the new wooden floor and built the garage round the fuselage and stubby wing roots. I wondered, *Will it fit? Can it be moved sufficiently to remove the enormous engine? Will the long tail survive being exposed to the elements?*

* * *

First Flight

A few years later, I'm talking to a real aeroplane. All that aluminium, wood, canvas, steel, and brass has come together for a first flight. This has not been a straightforward rebuild like the Velocette motorcycle; given all the rules and regulations, it has been an anguished dream of a rebuild. My new main spar is fine, but the corroded surrounds are causing concern for the Civil Aviation Authority (CAA). The bits of my aeroplane found in fields and farms in Ayrshire are being married to sophisticated French pieces from Plessis Belleville and Livry Gargan.

I don't know anyone who has flown this type of aeroplane, so I've built a cardboard simulator in my bedroom. I sit there on the carpet on a narrow aeroplane bucket seat and look at my cardboard-cut-out aeroplane. Over my chaise longue, I can see the garden with shaped bushes, curves and verticals, tone, colour, texture – it's a virtual reality show. I'm tempted to make aeroplane noises, but instead, I close my eyes and try to remember the various moves.

1. Pull starter and start up.
2. Check that oil pressure is rising.
3. Ensure that cut-off air valve is closed.

The compressor valve opens and the fuel pump is off. It still feels funny to be sitting on the carpet and rehearsing a flight. I try to imagine the whole first flight. I can imagine starting the engine because I've done that before. But what about the pre-take off checks?

I need a list. Take off, 50 knots; climb at 90 knots; cruise 120 knots; downwind checks; finals; and land; stop the engine, and close down. I try to get the picture. Through the bedroom window I hear a motorcycle putter gently down the Crescent.

Simulator on the Sofa

1 Fuel reserve closed.
2 Electric switches on as required.
3 Fuel on.
4 Prop. On fine, then automatic.
5 Fuel pump on.
6 Fuel pressure 200 to 300 gr/cm^2.
7 5 or 6 pumps of throttle depending on temperature after swinging the propeller.

8 Clear propeller.
9 Cut-off valve air cylinder on.
10 Magnetas on right and left.

But now it's for real. I'm going to make this flight on my own, put my money where my mouth is. It's taken so long for me to rebuild this Messerschmitt aeroplane. Built in 1947, it's fifty-eight years old in 2005. I think of all the corrosion and fatigue … and that's just the pilot! I feel happy with starting up and taxiing because I've practise this once or twice, but as I line up to take off, a voice from somewhere says, "Is this wise?"

I get permission for the circuits and taxi off. Here we go! I'm overwhelmed with joy and optimism. After a good, smooth take off, I've got to remember to keep the speed below 100 knots with the undercarriage down for this first circuit. I climb to 1,000 feet and turn onto the downwind leg, setting the power for about 70 knots. I balance the ball in the middle, and the aeroplane flies well, but the view from the cockpit is completely different from the planes I've flown before. Here you look down the side of the long nose. The left base leg follows, and I try to descend to make the runway. My rate of descent is gradual and careful. I see that I'm too high and wonder if I should extend the leg into a large S approach to work off the extra height, but in this unfamiliar aeroplane, I decide against it and lower the flaps fully to 40 degrees.

The plane is going to overshoot a bit, so I take off the power enough to glide to the numbers at the threshold of the runway. I keep the speed at 65 knots. The plane quickly flares, drops, and bounces high. I open the throttle and go round again, bringing the flaps up as the plane reaches 300 feet. And then it's downwind and once again into the finals. My confidence is shattered, and this time I get a bit low and need more power. There's a 7 knot crosswind, and I ease into the wind by side slipping a little. The response from the old aeroplane is full-blooded, and I have to take off the sideslip quickly and flare at the same time. There's another bounce, and it's once more into the air for a third circuit. This time, with a bit more power, I get onto the runway without a big bounce, more a series of little bounces as the aeroplane runs along and then starts to pull to the left. *Has a tyre burst?* I muse. The plane continues to veer to the left, and I let her leave the runway and come to a halt on the grass. The port undercarriage is damaged and folding up. The aircraft has a list. The fire brigade members are on their way as I switch off the engine and see whether my dreams and fourteen years of work are shattered. I wonder, *Is this the first and last flight?*

Back to the Floor of the Shed like the Wright Brothers

I return to the floor of my shed, the scene of so much rebuilding and struggling with bits and pieces. It still has a patina of aeroplane paint from the early, heroic days. It reminds me of those two naked pilots, Wilbur and Orville Wright. In 1900, the big thing among young men in Dayton, Ohio, was owning and running a buggy and team of horses. The Wright brothers, however, built sheds out in the sands of Kitty Hawk on the Grand Banks on the North Carolina coast. There, the wind was steadiest and strongest in the whole of the United States. It was a bit like deciding to go out on the machair in Islay to put up a frail, wooden shed, which was transported to the island by a Clyde puffer. Year after year, Wilbur and Orville took timber, repaired the shed after winter storms, and built a home for a new glider that they learned to control before even thinking of flying themselves. Perhaps their expertise in building sheds was the first move towards powered flight.

My own shed in Skelmorlie gave me a lot of trouble. The aeroplane tail stuck out through a five-foot hole in the end wall, weakening the integrity of the structure. I left a handful of four-inch nails and a hammer for emergencies. During January storms, I had to hold on to the shed, hammering nails into any loose timber I could find to keep the walls upright. The aluminium fuselage of the aeroplane would otherwise have been ripped out of the shed by the wind and blown in the direction of Rothesay. Later, I strutted the corner of the shed with a massive four-inch by two-inch beam, attaching the shed to the house with a metal tie, all in an effort to reduce the shed's self-destructive movements to and fro.

Wilbur, how did you ever manage to leave your glider at Kitty Hawk over the winter? And how did you find it again unharmed when you came back in the spring? I think kids would learn about the miracle of flight best by standing inside a wooden shed during a gale and feeling the force of nature before returning to the classroom to look at the model of the Wright brothers' glider.

The floor space in the shed in Skelmorlie now has the Velocette LE on its stand in the middle of the floor. Aeroplane and spare engine have been launched into the blue. A parcel arrives with the Christmas post: the new stainless steel exhaust pipes for the

Velocette motorcycle. During the last trial on the stop and start LE, I felt as though something was hindering the engine. When I needed power for the hills, something wasn't quite right. Running down to Lunderston Bay, I tried to hold onto 45 mph and detected a kind of surge as the engine cleared itself. *Could the rusty old pipes and silencer be blocked?* Even a partial blockage would cause a back pressure enough to stifle the small engine. I thought it was worth a try to replace them.

I love creative working spaces, preferably adapted. I love old schools, photographers' studios, barns, byres, cottages, and the like. I think it has something to do with the quality of the seriousness of purpose. Ann Livingston and I bought a wonderful school in Aberdeenshire in 1969: Fetternear School and Schoolhouse. It has haunted my dreams ever since. We started so many creative things there. There was even a ghost of a creative school dominie who had died young, full of ideas and dreams to develop but frustrated by illness. His was a kind of benign presence, and he seemed to sympathise with my odd ideas. He would occasionally make his presence felt. He chose the same place every time. As I closed the garage door on a dark night, he would place his cold hand over mine. The hairs on the back of my neck still stand on end when I think about it.

The picture of Wilbur Wright in his leanto shed is fascinating. "Working long hours every day in his leanto, slowly and with infinite pains, Wilbur put his machine together. For each wing, he formed an oblong with the spars, then filled in with the ribs, spacing them about a foot apart. An essential part of the design was simple strength of construction to reduce the chance of the machine's coming apart in the air when buffeted by strong winds or of sustaining damage in a rough landing. To this end, he worked with great care, actually testing each single piece of wood and every metal fitting from the tiniest to the largest that went into the machine.

'This meticulous workmanship of Wilbur's was a personal ideal that was foreign to nearly every other experimenter of the time, and it contributed in no small measure to his eventual success. He was never to abandon this ideal of confident self-reliance, this desire to see with his own eyes, to feel with his own hands, to accept nothing on trust, to check and recheck. Even by itself, this was an approach that set him apart from such men as Maxim and Langley, who were mainly thinkers supplying designs to be constructed for them by hired workmen. In later years, when Wilbur had finally brought the aeroplane before the eyes of the world, this attitude was never relaxed, and his everlasting, answerable attention to detail became amazement to everyone who was allowed to be near him." [6]

Wilbur's shed masterpiece was the one he built in 1901. He designed a structure seven feet high by sixteen feet by twenty-five feet with a low-pitched roof that was built of plain board on the sides and hung on a framework of two-by-fours. A nice touch allowed both end walls to be swung out and up on hinges and propped open. Alongside the shed, the living quarters would be in a tent. Orders for the shed lumber, cut to size, were sent ahead with directions to forward it to Kitty Hawk.

What a story! In my shed at Skelmorlie there is a space where the spare engine for my aeroplane once sat in the middle of the floor. A space must be filled, so just this year, my Velocette is filling it. I pulled the bike out of the dog kennel, and it's much easier to work on in this larger space. Fit the new exhaust pipes, lubricate the speedometer cable, hoist the front end, remove the front wheel, clean and grease the wheel bearings, and clean and adjust the brakes. The various aeroplane parts have a wonderful dialogue with the Velocette's honest Birmingham engineering, and I fumble through the maintenance, blow the tyres up, and check the oil levels. Now is the time.

This must have been the feeling Wilbur and Orville had in 1902. Their first sight of the swing-door shed was depressing. The ends sagged, the roof sagged, and the winter winds had blown away the foundations. The best-laid plans of mice and men gang aft agley, and it took them weeks just to make the shed liveable. But by 8 September 1902, they could start and assemble their new glider. The real hour was during Friday on 10 October 1902. With his vision of controlled flight, Wilbur utilised his invention of the moveable rudder to coordinate the turns with the banking of the wings. Every pilot owes this "ball in the middle" realisation of flight to Wilbur and Orville.

Every time I flew the Nord, this was my first priority. It took quite an effort to balance and fly the old aeroplane well. The ball in the middle is the simplest instrument on an aeroplane; it's the same as a spirit level or level finder because it shows the out-of-balance pressure clearly and instantly. All the followers of Wilbur have to do is press the rudder in the direction indicated. Easy, isn't it?

I'm thinking of the motor the Wright brothers put together for their High Noon at Kitty Hawk. I think it developed roughly the same horse power as the flat, twin engine on the Velo. Mind you, there are only fifty years between them!

Wilbur's motor, developed from a car engine with a curious name, the Pope Toledo, made 12 bhp, but it fell back to 9 bhp. when the valves got hot.

My state-of-the-art 1948 motorcycle is the same horizontally opposed design as The Wright Flyer. This means that the carburettor sits in the middle of a long induction pipe between the cylinders (which, on later models, was actually heated from the radiator). I remember replacing the carburettor and had to use an unheated pipe, which certainly worked well in the summer. My high noon is, unfortunately, in the middle of winter, and this affects the running of the motorcycle. I frantically push and pull the choke slide, which helps a bit. The small light engine runs well on steady settings, and once started, I decide not to stop at the Crescent. The road between Skelmorlie and Cornalees Bridge is twisty and steep. I'm riding the Velo up a slippery slope behind a large, black

4x4. It's freezing cold, and the engine doesn't like anything other than a steady throttle setting, so I get very close to the 4x4. My brightly painted machine persuades the driver of the 4x4 that I am impatiently trying to overtake, but the truth is that a notice inside the lid of the Velo's toolbox reads, "Do not exceed 35 mph in second gear." The worried woman pulls over into a passing place and waves me on. The roads are mostly single track with passing places, and I get into a good rhythm, making the most of the motorcycle's narrow width. The roads are heavily frosted, but only occasionally covered with ice. It reminds me of the original *Motor Cycling Magazine* road test by Mr Osborne of the LE Velocette. This was carried out in four inches of snow, giving Mr Osborne "no trouble whatsoever owing to the good handling of the Velocette." Ah! 1955!

I find an unused ferry ticket in my pocket. Can I take a chance on Le Velo? Can I cross the Firth of Clyde to Hunter's Quay and celebrate the New Year at the Coylet Hotel on Loch Eck? Western Ferries have sympathy for old bikes. Over the years, I've travelled with them in all sorts of weather, and I suppose the bikes have become quainter and odder with time. Somehow, one is left with the unusual and offbeat, the more expensive bikes are sold as the need arises.

A slight stuttering of the Velocette is cured by simply keeping the old high-tension leads to the spark plugs away from metal contacts because there seems to be some shorting going on. On the ferry, the air is clear and cold. I left the pudding top helmet and goggles at home and brought a full-face helmet instead, but it is so cold that the visor hazes over with breath. I build a rhythm riding the bike: visor clean, change gear, throttle back, hand change, visor clean, hand brake. All that hand waving keeps me warm. It's difficult to tell black ice from shining black tar on the narrow roads. I cruise past Ardnadam Sandbank; Dalinlongart; Strone; Ardbeg; Kilmun; Ardentinny; Whistlefield and Coylet. It's like the history of Scotland passing me by.

It's getting really cold and my fingertips are freezing. I just hope the Coylet Inn is open. It is, and I'm able to warm up near the roaring fire. I sup my soup, drink my Guinness, and impatiently wait for the main course. The manager of the hotel was a biker in his younger days, and over the meal, he tells me stories of driving sixty miles to Birmingham and back, every day to work. Thirty thousand miles covered in less than a year, in all types of weather. Just outside the window, there is a surreal view of four palm trees shining greenly against the black water of the loch. They look to be having a conversation as they sway in the breeze – a bit like the conversation I had with a motorcycle enthusiast on the ferry until he retired to the warmth of his car. Palm trees are a feature of this part of the west coast; it has something to do with the Gulf Stream. After the meal to welcome 2009, I decide to warm up a bit by walking up Puck's Glen, which is a few miles from the Coylet. There's nothing like a steep crumbling Scottish path to get the circulation going. Puck's Glen is a kind of like Hollywood with its palm trees, but it looks very beautiful with its new Japanese bridges that cross the gorge of the glen. The winter light is fading, and it's time to start back for Hunter's Quay at Dunoon. The air is wonderfully cold with a kind of pine ozone quality that the motorcycle preserves the skin against.

On the ferry back to Sandpoint, the bike won't start on the hand-start, but once the ferry is empty, I can run and jump and push the bike into life, and then I can burble through the gloaming in style.

I push the Velocette straight into the shed, among the aeroplane parts. *I wonder, is there any Bowmore whisky left?*

Naked Pilots: William Burns, Amy Johnson, and Antoine de Saint-Exupéry

Naked Pilot started it all. My exhibition opened in the Collins Gallery in Glasgow in 1993. This was a renaissance for me, and I wanted a renaissance exhibition. Could I put together all my dreams and anguish? Would all the different directions of my life somehow pause in space and dance to my tune?

The *Naked Pilot* was a wonderful focus for the twentieth century. My staring eyes were focused on three pilots: Bill Burns, a Scottish artist and teacher who was based in Aberdeenshire. He was head of art at Aberdeen College of Education. He disappeared in his own aeroplane on 14 October 1972. Amy Johnson – wonderful Amy – gained worldwide fame for her amazing aerial journeys, and she set new records as she went. She disappeared on 5 January 1941. Antoine de Saint-Exupéry did everything; he was a writer, magician, raconteur, and pilot. He left the world *The Little Prince* and ended his life as the oldest fighter pilot of the Second World War. He disappeared on 31 July 1944.

> "I've put something there that wasn't there before," Bill Burns said. "I'll just go over the top of the weather," said Amy Johnson. "J'admire le science, bien sur, mais j'admire aussi la sagesse." said Antoine de Saint-Exupéry.

The first naked pilot I'll examine is William Burns, RSA, RSW, DA (Glasgow). He flew in the Second World War and was wounded. His rehabilitation options included crochet, knitting, and painting. He attended Glasgow School of Art and Hospitalfield Arbroath. He taught in: Dunoon, Edinburgh and Aberdeen College of Education. He flew for the RAF (1939–1942), and he flew light aircraft later (1938–1972). His painting was seen in the Glasgow School of Art (1948), Edinburgh, Manchester, Dundee, Newcastle, and the National Gallery of Canada.

The pilot, a stumpy, aggressive figure in a leather flying jacket, leaves the flying club and walks over to his aircraft, which is parked beside the Tay. It is a raw October day. Low clouds seem to weigh heavily on the slender fuselage and wings of his aeroplane.

He takes off, straight as a die, balanced and expert, heading north, following the coast, homeward bound. Images flood into his mind.

Burns once said, "The other day, I was flying at 3,000 ft, towing a glider. A nylon rope about 100 ft long is fixed to my aircraft on a quick-release hook under the rudder operated from the cockpit, and attached to the glider by a nose hook, also quick-release from the glider cockpit. All will be well as long as both pilots know what they are doing, but on this particular day, I was towing a new boy on his first ever aerotow. He did not keep station during a climbing turn and wrapped the nylon rope around my rudder and elevators. Pulling my glider release did nothing to help, as the rope was now firmly attached to the entire tail assembly. The glider pilot should have pulled his release, although I still would have been in big trouble. But being new, he panicked and put the nose down. This brought my tail down and stalled the aircraft. My aircraft began to spin. With no rudder or elevators, there was nothing I could do. I don't wear a parachute, but the glider pilot did, and by this time, he had used it. So as they used to say in the RAF days, there was I with nothing on the clock but the maker's name and the maker's name was Smith. I switched off the engine, shut off the petrol supply, then took my feet off the rudder and jammed them against the instrument panel The hideous noise of the flying wires and the constant whirling of the fast-approaching earth were sickening, and every so often the glider would jerk the aircraft partially out of its spin and into a dreadful yawing movement not to be found in any aerobatic manual. The glider hit first, and my machine went in on one wing, acting as a huge shock absorber which probably saved my life. The engine ended up under my legs as I had anticipated, but the aircraft did not catch fire. Someone put a mask over my face in the ambulance, and at the moment, I am being fed soup by the most attractive nurse you could possibly imagine. She has a marvellous head. In fact, it's familiar, it's Modigliani's Elvira. Wonderful! The shape is so aesthetically perfect it could not be bettered." [10]

The low stratus uncoils on both sides of the aeroplane. The coast eases out of the mist in unfamiliar shapes that are only recognisable as they disappear beneath the nose; cliffs; bays; villages; headlands; strange lines in the sea and strange marks on the fields. He calls his home aerodrome and gives an estimated time of arrival. He's cleared to the inbound lane to Portlethan and Aberdeen Harbour. The haar (*Scottish mist)* becomes thicker and more opaque. He slows the aircraft and gets lower to keep the cliffs in sight. He's losing sight now of all his references. The goldfish bowl is closing in on him. He suddenly feels he can't go on. "Return to Dundee 180° to head south," he says. Watch the instruments, move the stick and rudder, watch the altitude. This is no image; this is no dream; this is for real. Turn and turn, and turn. The machine goes in on one wing into the North Sea.

Press & Journal, Monday 16 October 1972, Artist–Pilot Is Lost at Sea

The well-known north-east artist and academician, Mr William A Burns, is missing and presumed dead after a weekend plane crash. The plane he was piloting, a single-engine Fournier, plunged into the sea in dense fog between Newtonhill and Portlethan, and then it broke up. A Navy minesweeper, HMS Brinton, assisting police, coastguards, and Aberdeen lifeboats in the search, recovered the wings and tail about 300 yards offshore. The wreckage was taken to the Navy base at South Queensferry. Mr Burns' body was not recovered, and yesterday the search was called off.

Mr Burns (fifty-one) an ex-RAF pilot and experienced flyer was a bachelor. He lived alone at Grinaan, Whitecairns, and Balmedie. He was returning on a solo flight from Dundee to Aberdeen on Saturday night when he got into difficulty. Mr Biggs at 13 Betridge Road, Newtonhill saw the plane just before six o'clock in the evening. He said yesterday, "I had seen the plane moving into a bank of mist. From the noise he seemed to be throttling down and trying to wheel back into the land. At this point, I couldn't see the plane, but I could hear the engine. The noise suddenly stopped, and there was the sound of an impact." Mr Burns, a member of Aberdeen & District Flying, bought the Fournier three years previously. Mr Burns, who was born in Glasgow, was principal lecturer and head of the art department at Aberdeen College of Education. He trained at Glasgow School of Art and at Hospital Art Trust, Arbroath. Shortly after going to Aberdeen in the early fifties, he was elected an associate of the Royal Scottish Academy. He was elected an academician in 1970.

Jimmy Scotland, Principal of Aberdeen College of Education, wrote:

W. A. BURNS

Bill Burns, who disappeared in the middle of October during a flight from Dundee to Aberdeen, was a very distinguished artist and those who have written about him rightly stressed this part of his work. It should not be forgotten that he was also that rarest of creatures, an inspirational teacher. I knew him only as a trainer of teachers and in that role he had some critics who saw him as dogmatic, over-radical, and sometimes downright rude. His standards were extremely high and he was not prepared to put up with anything less than total effort. If he thought a man was wrong or lazy, he never hesitated to tell him so to his face. And when, like everyone else on occasion, his judgement was wrong, he was less prepared than most to acknowledge that it might be. He made few allowances. Even on philosophical points of education theory he argued like a panzer division.

That was one side of Burns, some people never saw another. But there was much more. He became head of the art department in Aberdeen College of Education, and his teacher training was the best I have seen after a quarter of a century of teacher training. The courses in arts and crafts were his creation – so were the main art studies in the primary diploma course. He always maintained that, "The informed primary teacher is the person to teach art in the primary school." And he believed that teachers could help students develop their own talents. The work they produced under his guidance was impressive. Contrary to some people's impressions, he was not always arguing; rather, he had a keen sense of humour and clever way of speaking, often using Scottish idioms. He did not make many friends, but he grappled them to his soul with hoops of steel. And he had the rarer faculty of making disciples.

Two years before he died, he resigned his post in the Aberdeen College. It was quite a wrench. He once told me that, for the first few months after he left us, he woke up every morning and planned his college work for the day. He certainly never intended that his separation from teaching would be permanent; he hoped that, in a year or two, he would head back to school.

The sudden, dramatic manner of his death was somehow in the pattern of a man like Bill Burns, but it was (and is) distressing nonetheless. Not only Scottish art, but Scottish art teaching suffered a grievous loss.

Bill Burns Painting by James Hardie, 1977

Bill Burns learned to fly with the Glasgow Flying Club in 1938. The RAF claimed him during the outbreak of war, and he flew on active service until 1942. After various trials and errors, he attended Glasgow School of Art from 1944 to 1948. He bought his own aeroplane after a successful show at the Scottish Gallery during the 1968 Edinburgh Festival. He flew regularly and kept his aeroplane in its own hangar at Dyce, Aberdeen. His Fournier RF4, built in Czechoslovakia, didn't have any blind-flying instruments (no gyrocompass or artificial horizon, for instance). It was more of a single-seater powered glider than a light aircraft. He loved to fly low, and he often flew over his friends' houses in expert fashion, presenting his characteristic silhouette at the windscreen.

Private Pilot's Licence and Learning to Fly

When Bill Burns learned to fly in the late thirties, his instructors were swashbuckling former pilots from the Royal Flying Corps (whose generation made up the first fighter pilots in the world). The First World War had ended only twenty years before Burns took up flying. Flying instructors are all different. The modern Civil Aviation Authority (CAA) members are quite right to emphasise *character* as the baseline in safe flying. Somehow, the character of the instructor comes through the formula of teaching the basics of flying and the various hurdles to getting a pilot's licence.

There are so many stories about the instructor–student relationship. You have to be lucky to find something in the teaching that touches your imagination. My luck was Peter Forbes of Pegasus Flying Club in Aberdeen in 1969. Peter said he hated flying ever since he had to parachute out of aeroplanes in the Second World War. That was because he was in the British Airborne and associated flying with the worst and most terrifying moments of his life. He was a very handsome cavalier of a man in his sixties. And despite his age, he courted a beautiful Aberdonian 18-year-old woman named Moira with all the panache he brought to his flying club where he was the chief flying instructor.

I was a lecturer in art at Aberdeen College of Education. I was married with two children and had long given up any youthful ideas of being a pilot. However, on Christmas in 1969, my wife, Ann Livingston, gave me a trial flying lesson voucher for Pegasus Flying Club, Dyce. I presented myself on Boxing Day at the door of the flying club caravan, and I was greeted by Peter Forbes like a long-lost brother.

Peter was a dry-cleaner with shops in Perth and Kirkwall on Orkney. He had learned to fly in his sixties with the imaginative idea of dividing his time between the two shops. He also had a kind of longing for the control and discipline he had learned as a paratroop major. He explained to me that he was full of bullshit, but he liked the look of me. I reminded him of his younger brother, who was an artist, and he liked the idea of having an artist in his club. I explained I could only afford flying lessons when I sold a painting, but this appealed to him even more, and he said we'd talk about money some other time.

Propellers Painting by James Hardie, 2003

It was the start of a breathless, frightening time when I learned to fly in the north-east of Scotland with mountains, high winds, and strange weather due to the fact that the Atlantic met the cold North Sea there.

My lessons were structured around stories of how to meet women, how to leave women, and how retired "pirates" like him could never be satisfied. I went solo after eight and a half hours – somewhere between meeting women and leaving women. How he became a retired "pirate" took care of my cross-country exercises, and my flying test was really the story of his divorce.

I thought it was absolutely wonderful, the only way to teach flying! Peter's moods and optimism saw me through crosswind landings and on to cross-country exercises. I remember one very well. I think I had about twenty hours of total flying time at that point. On a beautiful morning filled with luminous sunshine and the sly weather of the North East, Peter and I set off from Dyce. I flew the aeroplane exactly as he instructed me. We climbed to 3,000 ft, which he showed me on the altimeter, and we climbed steadily at 70 knots.

As we did a climbing turn to follow the coast north, I noticed some grey, woolly stuff that Peter instructed me to go through and level off when we got to 3,000 ft. We headed north about 15 ml. to the conspicuous Ythan Estuary. Here, I practised turns and stalls. I was suffused with delight and enthusiasm. We then steered 260 degrees back to Dyce, still at 3,000 ft. I called in that we were approaching Dyce from the north and wanted joining instructions. Peter kept up his colourful commentary about his women: we were on the downwind leg with a beautiful redhead he met in Hamburg.

When we landed, we were met with a surprise. "I'd like you to go off on your own, Jim, and do all that again just as we did it." He leapt out of the two-seater and murmured, "Moira" before I went into the deep blue.

"Climb to 3,000 ft and turn north over the coast, but this time there seems to be more of the woolly stuff, but just go through it, old chap. It's nothing to a man of your calibre."

Soon, I was flying up north to the Ythan Estuary, where I forgot all about Dyce due to the extreme concentration I needed to fly the little aeroplane and perform turns and stalls. The light glinted off aluminium and Perspex, creating a little world of its own in the enormous sky. Turning and turning was almost mesmeric and disorientating. Enclosed in the cabin, one only saw a bit of the ground and horizon at a time.

I only knew three instruments: air speed indicator, altimeter, and gyrocompass (set from the real compass on the ground and checked from time to time in the air). I was good at checks and had memorised them: fuel, radio, engine, DI, altimeter (FREDA). I thought she was a dark-haired woman, like the one Peter had met in Brussels.

I then thought, *Turn 260 degrees and make the radio calls to Dyce.* I was thinking about field in sight when I realised that a huge, dark curtain had appeared from the South and stretched from far above me to far below me. Peter must have decided this was a test to see whether I had the right stuff, so on I sailed at 3,000 ft.

The fluffy stuff had multiplied, and somehow, it devoured the whole sky. The greys ranged from the palest to the darkest, and they seemed wickedly solid. Little bells rang in my overfilled mind: *Is this not called flying into cloud?*

Propellers Painting by James Hardie, 2003

I had read so many stories about flying that I thought such a situation could be fatal unless one believed one's instruments. I looked at the instruments, and they looked back at me.

In his unusual way, Peter had shown me how to deal with extreme puzzlement in the air. He said, "Take your hands and feet off the controls and see what this little training aeroplane will do."

I remembered his instructions and followed them. Unfortunately, in dense cloud, the sounds of the engine change according to how dense the cloud is. This makes you feel like the aeroplane is changing direction and height. I started to sweat. Alone in the cockpit, hardly able to see the wing tips of the plane; I had to take decisive action. I had to make a 180-degree turn to exit the huge cloud bank and return to the much desired Ythan Estuary.

Gently, I touched the rudder, and little by little, I eased the aeroplane into a right-hand turn that was more of a yaw. I didn't know what an artificial horizon was and didn't really want to look at the instruments. It felt like it took a year to make the turn, and in fact, it took about a year to recover from the fright fully. I actually thought I might never fly again. And Bill Burns' reaction was memorable when he looked me in the eye and muttered, "There you are Jim - you know you've got what it takes; you're lucky."

Flying Adventures with Bill Burns

Peter would phone me from time to time once I'd gotten my pilot's licence. "Could you take two engineers from Perth to Kirkwall to service the dry-cleaning machines?" We stayed the night with one of Peter's girlfriends, a brunette, and we serviced the machines and returned the next day. The weather always springs a surprise, but never quite like my first big surprise. I enjoyed moving to plan B and successfully thinking out routes to get the quiet, sensible men back to Perth. They always asked Peter if I could fly them; they knew a lucky idiot when they saw one.

Peter told me to get my priorities right: "Never leave the keys in the aeroplane. People you haven't quite paid might get the nasty idea of stealing them. Then where will you be?"

I remember one hilarious flight to Inverness Flying Club where I was sent on a mission to recover a carpet that Peter felt was his. I duly unlocked the club door and rolled up the carpet, hoping it wasn't as big as it looked. The rolled up carpet had to be threaded through the window and into the back of the Cessna. Optimistically, I had invited a colleague from the college of education to help with the carpet, but I didn't have a spot for him to sit.

The electric starter was flat, so not only did he have nowhere to sit but he had to hand-start the thing. Of course, he was a talented musician with very important hands and I had a terrible vision of a backfire with dreadful consequences. I shut off the ignition, and a few pull-throughs were enough to persuade the electrics to come alive and start the engine and whirl the propeller. David was small and made no protests about curling himself gratefully round the carpet. He would still be able to play the piano after the ordeal.

Bill Burns had taken me up on my first flight in the summer of 1969. He was a bit peculiar, and if the person hesitated over his offer and felt nervous that seemed to excite him and cause him to press them to fly with him. With my enthusiasm, I came very far down the list, but eventually, he couldn't resist sharing the experience, and I took to the air in a tiny Messerschmitt-Bölkow for the first time. He was very tense and worried about the damage I might cause as I folded my large frame into the footholds, handholds, and seat. "Hand," he said, and I moved my hand. "Foot," he said, and I moved my large foot. "Sit," he said, and I sat. The wings were set about shoulder height, and they reminded me of Stonehouse chute, which dived down a steep hill. The glass canopy was described as very fragile and only worked if an expert was there to close it. The control column was in the centre of the aeroplane along with the throttle. I had difficulty imagining the rest of the aeroplane, and it felt like a strange dentist's chair, especially when the shrill engine started up.

It was very impressive wearing earphones for the first time and hearing the completely unintelligible radio telephone. The speed built up very quickly, and up in the air I wondered where the speed went. The higher we climbed, the less of an impression of speed I had until we seemed to be perched in the air with the fields, farms, and roads slowly moving past us. "We're doing 90 knots." We flew steadily along with alarming bursts of radio through the ear phones and a glittering display outside the Perspex.

I just couldn't make sense of the view and wondered where Aberdeen was. We had to be pointing at something before it materialised. There were strange shapes and colours before I recognised the Ythan Estuary.

Suddenly, the whole world tilted in an alarming way. It was as if the wing fell off or I put my foot through something vital. It was only a gentle turn, though, and we smoothly came back to straight and level as my ex-fighter pilot said while pointing at the interesting things to see. It took a lot of looking to make sense of them, but once identified, the details were clear.

Suddenly, I'm warned about a steep turn. *What's that-* I muse; I find out the whole world tips and keeps tipping until the horizon is vertical. I look over my shoulder, and there's Stonehouse chute dropping away into the void. "Don't panic," says the voice through the ear phones as I try to crawl in the opposite direction of the void. *Oh my God!* Life would never be the same. As I wrote for my film, *The First Aerial Voyage in Scotland 1795.*

DOUBTER; "If the good Lord wanted us to fly, He would have given us wings"

BELIEVER; "If He wanted us to stay on the ground, He would have given us roots."

"I'll Just Go over the top of the Weather"
Amy Johnson

In my *Naked Pilot* exhibition, my most vulnerable dreamer was Amy Johnson. The exhibition travelled to the Ferens Gallery Hull, (Amy's home town) in 1994, and somehow, I came as near as I ever will to all these different directions making a pause in space. Amy became a public figure and raised the dreams and hopes of thousands in the thirties. What I couldn't believe was the enormous amount of envy that accompanies this daring-to-do dream. People saw her as the classic British heroine; people saw her as a gold-digger; people saw her as a slut. What is it in human nature that allows for such contrary notions to exist in a person's mind? Everyone wears masks.

My favourite painting is Amy wearing three masks perched on top of my Nord 1101. She has a sexy, leather-and-fur flying coat, cool goggles, and a leather helmet. The other side of the coin is a painting of Amy and her husband, Jim Mollison, after their crash in July 1933. Jim Mollison pressed on to New York, flying their De Havilland Dragon Rapide. Amy's instinct urged her to land when the fuel indicated empty, but they were so near. The crash was serious, and Jim was seriously injured. A friend of mine, Tom Crawford from Port Banntyne, said Jim Mollison was never the same again. I painted Jim and Amy several times with bandages and Elastoplasts.

Three Faces of Amy Johnson by James Hardie, 1992

Using my old aeroplane to kick-start art was exciting. When I was dismantling the plane in the shed/garage/hangar in the garden, I tried an exhibition of Saint-Exupéry: *The Pilot, Planet and the Rose.* And I also tried an exhibition on Wilber and Orville Wright, *Wilber.*

This is why when, asked whether I was obsessed by the rebuilding of the aeroplane, I said *no.* The dismantling was as creative as any other part of the operation.

Declan Curtis in Prestwick

Eventually, I found a pilot who had a similar enthusiasm for old aeroplanes. His name was Declan Curtis. I became *Jasus Jim* as in, "Jasus, Jim, keep the ball in the middle or you'll kill us both!" Declan was a commercial pilot and founded Caledonian Chipmunks at Prestwick.

His flying and aerobatics in the Chipmunk gave him the necessary experience for the Nord 1101, and Declan solved the problems of the landing speed and people's attitudes regarding those who dare. All this was done at Prestwick, our home airport.

It was so interesting to think that Amy's last flight started at Prestwick in 1941. Her Airspeed Oxford was at Prestwick, waiting for the Air Transport Auxiliary (ATA), First Officer Amy Johnson, to ferry it to Blackpool and on to RAF Kidlington near Oxford. "I'll just go over the top of the weather," was how she summed it up on 5 January 1941.

It's a big jump to make use of such blind flying instruments, especially when I only had a dozen hours of flying time under my belt. Eventually, I took an *Instrument **Meteorological** Conditions* (IMC) rating when I moved from Aberdeen to a wonderful job in the Glasgow School of Art in 1980 and joined the club I'm still in (Prestwick Flight Centre).

The instrument flying of 1980 was very different than the "over the weather" flying of 1941. Today, there is abundant help from air traffic controllers in an emergency. 1941 was just after the Battle of Britain, and there was strict radio silence and not much interest in ferry flights.

How on earth did she arrive over the Thames Estuary when she was aiming at Oxford, which was 50 ml. away? But it happened all the time. Luftwaffe pilots would land in Cornwall, convinced they were on the Cherbourg Peninsula. I wondered, *will I be able to ferry my old aeroplane home without getting lost?*

Second Ferry Flight with René Mayer in Paris

The time had come to ferry the Nord home to Scotland the opposite way from Amy's flight in 1941. The port undercarriage had collapsed. The shock had been well contained in an alloy H bracket that had broken cleanly, allowing the undercarriage to fold but keep the wheel on the tarmac. Some damage had been done to the undercarriage panels and the flaps had been scraped. A new bracket would have to be found.

Some years before, my second wife and I had made an expedition to Paris to collect a pair of wings and undercarriage. We towed a glider trailer and Monsieur René Meyer of Livry- Gargan near Paris found us the wings. They were hanging from the roof of his hangar in Plessis Belleville aerodrome.

René, who couldn't speak English, was an amazing character. He came from Alsace Lorraine. His elder brother flew for the Luftwaffe in the Second World War, and he flew the famous Focke-Wulf 190. René, much younger, joined L'Armee de L'Air_after 1945 and flew the Nord 1101. He was a fount of knowledge and sold me all the bits and pieces I needed, including the properly certified wings and undercarriage.

He didn't like the English or the Americans, but he couldn't quite work out what an ecossaise was. I had worked in France as a youth hostel warden years before, and René could just about work out what I was trying to say.

René lived with Odette in a large, detached house in Livry-Gargan. He had taken over the basement and installed a Messerschmitt 109 that he was rebuilding. His masterpiece was a Bleriot 14. This I saw in the hangar at Plessis. René was larger than life. The best story I heard about him was just after the Berlin Wall was demolished. This opened up East Germany to the aircraft recoveries and rebuilders. So off René went with a hired lorry and crane. He dug up all sorts of flattened brackets and parts and patiently beat them into shape.

What he was really after was a FW 190 as a tribute to his brother, who was still alive. At last, he heard of a FW 190 that had crashed in marshland and sunk completely below the surface. The pilot had bailed out. Odette was very much against all this digging up and retrieving – they were both well over 70. Odette owned everything and employed young Italian and Spanish maids to run the house. She looked with great suspicion (as only a French bourgeoisie woman can) at Scottish pilots and artists.

After all my flying lessons with Peter Forbes, I managed to speak poetry in French: "*Que tu est joli, que tu me semble belle, sans mentir si votre plumage si rapport a votre ramage … tu est le phoenix des hauts de la bois.*" It was enough to bring out a particle of sympathy for *ecosser les pois* (***écossais***).

René dug up his Focke-Wulf or what was left of it under a mass of solid peat mud. He retrieved all he could and drove slowly back to Odette. Inside the gates of his minor chateau, the cleaning process began. High-pressure hoses could hardly shift the hardened mud. Eventually, Odette ordered the mass of stinking mud out of her house and garden … and she ranted and railed at René every minute of the day. She asked why he didn't send it over to Scotland where all that mud would never be noticed.

But René was made of stern stuff and continued cleaning and hosing down the wreck. One fine morning, he began to dig out the cockpit, which was still intact to some degree. What happened next impressed Odette.

A skeletal hand suddenly thrust over the cockpit wall as the canopy broke away from the fuselage. The pilot hadn't bailed out! I'll draw a veil over what happened next between Odette and René, but let's hope the *Unteroffizier* found some peace and quiet wherever he rests now.

French Engineer and Nord 1101 Booker

My old Nord has come to Personal Plane Services, Booker. Tony Bianchi is doing the rebuild for the insurance company. He keeps up a stream of invective against any pilot who damages an aeroplane and thinks there should be a law for putting them down – no question!

I found it difficult to travel from Skelmorlie to Booker. I left with Ryanair from Prestwick to Stanstead at 5:00 a.m. for the flight at 6:45 a.m. I went from London to Marlow by train, and then I hired a car to get to Booker up in the Chilterns. I went all that way for ground checks, but nothing went very well until Tony got hold of a French engineer, Bernard, who had the right expression on his face and in true French style, reversed washers and seals and rebuilt the nose undercarriage. He could read the manuals, too, which were all in French. French engineering is very different than British and American.

It's a French engineer's *metier* to invent and improve the rough directions of the manual, not take it too seriously. He decides on grub screws, locking pins, and such essentials as he thinks they are needed.

René told me a story that illustrates such behaviour. He had rebuilt a Nord 1001 taildragger, that was very close to Willy Messerschmitt's original Me 108 design. The aircraft was as original as he could make it, right down to the coats of paint that were courtesy of *L'Armee de L'Air.*

His first flight was with an Inspector to get his permit to fly with The DGAC (the French CAA). He took off briskly from Plessis Belleville, but at 500 ft. The engine gradually and gracefully powered down. René frantically used all he had ever learned about fuel pumping and priming, but it made no difference. The inspector told him to turn in and land downwind, but René tried a circuit to land back into the wind. He badly undershot and wiped off his undercarriage in a ploughed field.

The throttle spindle was smooth (no splines), and the lever had only a smooth bracket fitting (very like a motorcycle foot-change lever without the splines). Once it slipped, it stayed slipped. The engineer's *metier* should have told him to drill and fit a lock bolt. It was back to the drawing board. Bernard brought his *metier* to the old Nord and found quite a few problems that he solved with élan.

Again, I wondered, *what is the landing speed?* Enter Jonathon Whaley, a famous pilot who very kindly granted the first permit to fly. He told me how to find the landing speed: "Fly to 3,000 feet, lower the undercarriage and the flaps, and stall the aeroplane. Note the airspeed. Add 130 per cent to this figure. It's so simple when you know how. The stalling speed was almost off the clock: almost 40 knots and 30 per cent of 40 is 12, so the landing speed is 52 knots. At 50 knots and a trickle of power, it lands really easily and is not much affected by crosswinds. Jonathon proceeded to demonstrate all this in masterly fashion, finding that the rate of sink was really a feature of my heavy plane.

At last, along came 14 March 2005. Enter Declan Curtis, who accompanied me down to Henley-on-Thames where the Royal Barge Pub put us up for the night. After an early night, we got up at 8:00 a.m. to head to the airstrip. The weather's not very good, but there's going to be a window of fair weather that should let us find Blackpool. There, we can stop and check out the fuel and oil.

After the hustle and bustle of the previous months, Booker early on a Saturday morning seemed strangely quiet. Personal Plane Services is locked up and our compressed air cylinder for starting the engine is outside the locked hangar doors along with the aeroplane. We can see a few faces waiting to see what's going to happen.

There is just enough air to bring us up to 20 hpa, enough for a cold start. Declan hardly believes me regarding the starting procedure. It takes five full movements of the yellow throttle after turning the propeller five times to prime this large, straight six engines. Open the valve, check the fuel pressure, turn on mags 1 and 2, and with two hands, pull the detente and the knob at the same time. The engine starts immediately and sounds quite wonderful. We're going from near Oxford to Blackpool to Prestwick, the reverse of Amy Johnson's ferry flight in 1941.

There's a slight drizzle over the hills, but it looks clearer to the north. Declan is flying the Nord, and I'm providing the information to run it. We soon get into the cruise with the propeller in coarse pitch enough to provide 80 hpa, 2,300 revs, and 120 knots. Scotland, here we come!

The flying conditions get better and better, and conspicuous places stand out (such as Silverstone, various airfields round Birmingham, and the big sheds at Hawarden and the Dee Estuary). We contact Blackpool and land. We taxi to the fuel depot, and as we pull up to refuel, all the paramedics' stream out of their building and give us a cheer. Declan and I look at each other, and it's only then that we realise what we've done. This is my first flight, so I feel I have to do the honours: I walk over to a control sign and wave at a man who is looking the other way. I suddenly realise I'm in a Luftwaffe flying suit and looking a bit oily though full of the momentous flight. I try to explain all this, but this Blackpudlian is very suspicious and doesn't understand my accent. "*Coom* through," he says and locks the security gate behind me. I am now in Blackpool town, outside the aerodrome.

To pay my landing fee, I have to walk along the street to the terminal building. Security is very suspicious of me – my height, my beard, my strange apparel, my funny accent. As I try to pay the fee, they send for more security men in case I become more excited.

"Where is this so called Messerschmitt you claim to have landed?" I mention my Irish friend Declan, and I am promoted to two more security men and a large Range Rover. We have to travel a fair distance before the Nord puts in an appearance. Declan appears mouthing on about nude fashion models in a hangar, but security decides it's all going to be too much trouble and let's go, guaranteed by the flying paramedics who are obvious enthusiasts and as mad as we are.

We take off for the second leg, Blackpool to Prestwick and the weather holds until we reach the borders. The Solway Firth's north shore has clouds right down to the deck. We fly east then back west looking for a break. It's not Loch Ryan, but Wigtown Bay, and the River Cree runs up the valley to Pinwherry. Therefore, we turn north to Turnberry and Prestwick. Declan gets permission for a flyover above the international airport that is modern Prestwick, and I think of Amy Johnson as we do rollovers at 500 ft and land to a champagne reception. That's the price of the total disbelief of the club members when they see Luftwaffe 14 on apron Echo in front of their clubhouse.

Sometimes things work out right enough.

Saint-Exupéry: "J'Admire La Science, Bien Sur Mais Aussi La Sagesse"

"J'admire le science, bien sur, mais j'admire aussi la sagesse."
Antoine de Saint-Exupéry

"Tangier, that little nothing of a town, was my first conquest. It was, you see, my first theft. Yes. Vertically at first and from so far off. Then during the descent, this flowering of meadows, plants, and houses. Up into that daylight I was bringing a sunken city warmed by the breadth of life. And suddenly, 500 m from the field, this marvellous discovery into a man on my own scale, who was really and truly my booty, my creation, my game. I had captured a hostage and Africa was mine. Two minutes later, on the grass, I was young, as though put down on some star where life begins again. In a new climate. On this ground under the sky I felt like a young tree. I stretched my flight strained muscles with a marvellous craving. I took long, flexible strides to unlimber from piloting, and I laughed at having rejoined my shadow on landing."

How well Saint-Exupéry describes the strange, unreal dimensions of flying. In the imagination, all these feelings live. I remembered Saint-Exupéry's books when trying to do my first film, *Telford by Air* using the old aeroplane.

Thomas Telford was born in the Scottish Borders. He left school at eight and was apprenticed to a stonemason. With complete dedication, he educated himself after work and became famous for his imaginative engineering. Completely without self-interest or self-projection, his image has never been established. One has only to think of Isambard Kingdom Brunel and the image of the Victorian Engineer photographed in front of massive ships chains in full possession of his world.

Telford seems to have been a great supervisory engineer taking on huge projects such as churches, bridges, harbours, canals, and viaducts. He was employed all over England. In Scotland, he was given the task of resurrecting the infrastructure of Scotland after the disastrous neglect following the 1745 Rebellion.

The Department of Fisheries commissioned him to build harbours. He was particularly interested in the modern idea of relating and harmonising his engineering with the landscape and coast. He talked of rhythms and patterns and imagination, not unlike Saint-Exupéry.

In 2006, Moray Council employed me as an artist to try to express Telford's approach by air. Real Artists Partnerships was formed by me and three other artists: Graham Rogers, Dave Martin, and Cavan Convery. My medium, of course, was the Nord 1101. I had managed, with the help of Cavan, to fit a camera into the floor of the aeroplane. This small camera was carefully installed in the 1950s-style landing light – the landing light bulb was removed and the camera set in its place. Unfortunately, it was right in the path of brown, muddy oil from the engine, and the whole floor of the aeroplane resembled the River Ganges during the monsoon season. The first film was seen through an oil film and was quite useless.

I had hoped to use the adjustment on the landing light through 70" to its forward position for landing, but it was impossible. *Why is every new idea such a problem?* I muse.

July 2007 was a kind of deadline to produce film for a ceremony at Craigellachie Bridge, and in June, the trials with the camera failed completely. On 22 June 2007, we were doing a display at Newtownards in Northern Ireland. The Nord took up two journalists, BBC, and *The Spectator*. This was the first time they had been in a Vintage aeroplane, and their ideas about flying were completely turned around.

It's something to do with the exposed chain and sprocket that works the flaps. I had to warn people not to get their jackets caught up in the sprocket or all my procedures could become compromised. Their article carried the headline,

"Propellers and Parachutes as Flying Goes Back to Basics."

The aeroplane flew and flew, and I did various checks, one of which meant crawling under the fuselage to inspect the fuel for contamination. The underside of the fuselage was covered with oil and muck, but flat on my back on the tarmac, I noticed there was a shiny, clean bit. Would you believe it? It was the glass cover of the landing light. In its retracted position (flush with the floor of the fuselage) somehow the oil left the glass absolutely immaculate

Aerodynamics and I'm sure Wilbur smiled!

Propeller and Goggles Painting by James Hardie, 2004

The next week, the weather was horrible. I was stuck in Prestwick waiting to fly to Inverness, which would be our base for *Telford by Air.* We had four sites to explore: Burghead Harbour, Cullen Harbour, Craigellachie Bridge, and Tomintoul Church. At last, the weather was better up north, but it was still foul at Prestwick. I would pick up the boys at Inverness and contact Lossiemouth for clearance to fly round the coast and up the Spey valley to Craigellachie and Tomintoul.

I got away at last - fly up to the Crinan Canal and then north up the Great Glen to Loch Ness and over to Dalcross. I hadn't been to Dalcross for years and I remembered doing my qualifying cross-country tests back in the seventies. These days, we need an agent, and I wonder whether I should try to hangar the aeroplane for a day or two. The prices astonish me, and I park on the grass near the flying club and meet the art team. The rain buckets down, but towards evening, out comes the sun and the late-evening light - nearly horizontal and that is just what we need.

Let creativity begin! What's this?

The owner of the Heilan Coo flying club objects to us taking pictures. He says he has spent thousands on aerial photography, and he objects to us on his patch. He has decided we don't have the certificates he has and calmly lets us know that the police and the CAA will be waiting our return if we go ahead. He says we're facing six months in jail and 5,000-pound fine.

I try to explain that we are three artists using my personal aeroplane as a medium. I say that, with fifteen years of art school training between us, we are investing a bit more than might be obvious at first. He shouts away in a strange Newcastle accent, and he advises us to let him do all the photography so that we won't land in jail. He then reports us to the CAA, and there is an enquiry later in the summer. However, the weather is here, and our great experiment will start. I remember old Peter saying that one must be determined to carry on flying.

Over the sea, the aeroplane flies steadily at 500 ft, which gives a good focus on the sea texture and the sea bottom. Mysterious shadows and the wonderful contrast and pattern of the breaking waves are quite the sight. The nearly horizontal light creates a terrific rhythm in the pattern of the crisp shadows, which lengthen as we turn up the River Spey.

Craigellachie Bridge is the only site I have been to on foot. It's just as well, though, because the 1813 bridge has a modern neighbour: a vast, concrete monstrosity. The Telford Bridge is cut at an unusual angle to the hillside, and it is beautifully sited. The Castle-like turrets at both ends are unmistakable. The River Spey turns and turns, and bridges pass quite frequently. I have the ordnance survey maps, but suddenly I see the turrets. We photograph it carefully, but we later find out that it is a copy of the Telford classic. We fly north and south, but it takes another flight before we get the right one. Nothing in flying ever seems to be straightforward - nothing can be taken for granted.

Saint-Exupéry went so far as to say:-

"The earth teaches us more about ourselves than all the books. Because it resists us. Man discovers himself when he measures himself against the obstacle."

There are so many obstacles. On our very first art flight, we were threatened by the police and the CAA. Plus, our oil was running out. The inverted engine on the Nord, a Renault 6 Q, had always leaked oil, but this time it was serious. I had used up all the oil I had brought with me. The oil consumption was something like three litres per hour. I went round Inverness Airport, but no piston engine oil is kept there – it's all turbo prop oil.

I got some help from the flying club: 3 litres of S80. But Prestwick was almost an hour and a half flight and I only had 8 litres in the 20-litre tank.

In Vol de Nuits' words, "Then everything began to sharpen. Crests, peaks grew razor sharp cutting into the hard wind like bowsprits. And it seemed to him that they were veering and drifting around like ships of the line taking up their battle stations. The air was suddenly powdered with dust which billowed softly like a veil along the snows. He looked back to see if, in case of need, there was still an avenue of escape behind him, and a shiver ran up his spine. The entire cordillera behind him was now in seething ferment. I'm lost!

From a peak just ahead of him, the snow suddenly began to rise; the fume of a white volcano. Then from a second peak slightly to the right. And one after another, all the peaks caught fire as though successfully touched by some invisible runner"

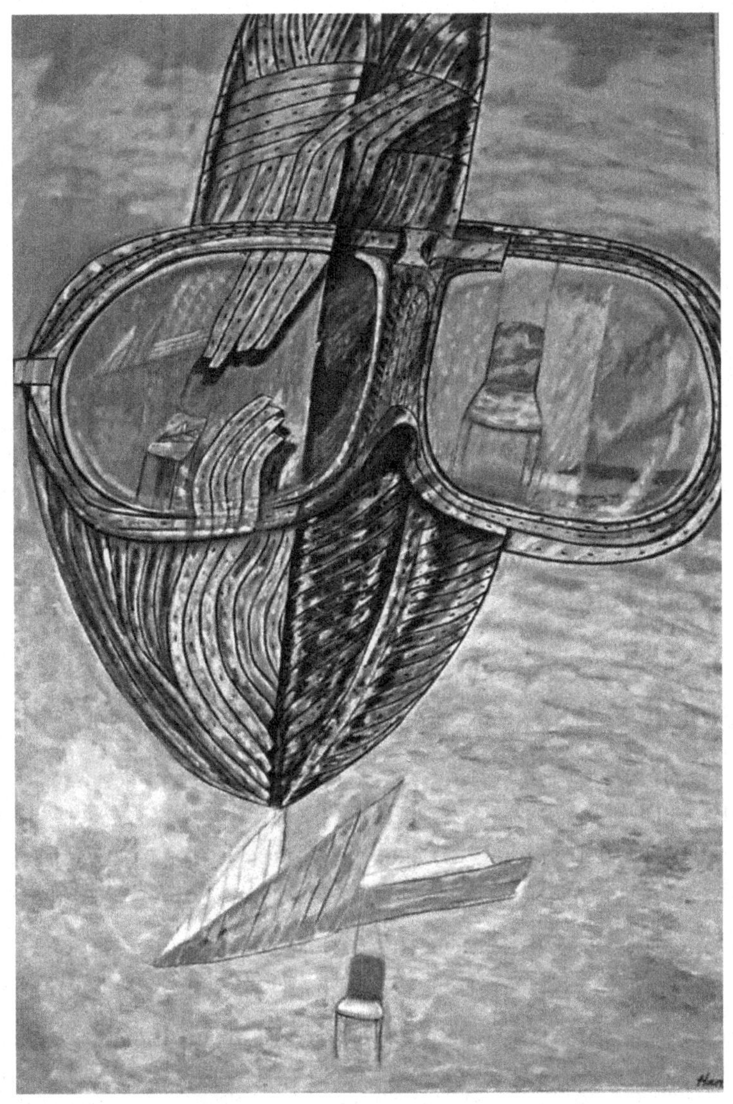

Artists Air Show Painting by James Hardie, 2004

The eerie world of Saint-Exupéry's transfiguration was soon going to be mine. Graham and I went in to Halfords in Inverness and bought a large can of motor oil for the older engine. At last, I had a fairly full tank of oil to try to get back to Prestwick.

At first, the weather was spectacular, but as I entered Loch Ness, great curtains of rain clouds folded in to the Great Glen. I eased underneath without gaining speed because the turbulence was quite bad and I remembered that my air frame was sixty years old.

Every Minute of the Shortest Flight (Detail) by James Hardie, 2009

When visibility is poor, such as when one is flying down a glen, one holds to one side to give the maximum turning space in case of the need for a 180-degree turn. The huge cloud formations towered up to 50,000 ft. There were massive dynamics that trembled the old wings as I flew south while holding my breath.

There is a strange, repeated pattern. The cloud moves diagonally across the wide glen just as an opening appears from the west, but it often slips away, across, and a clearing shows the ongoing Caledonian Canal and Lochs. Glen Garry is particularly bad this morning; in fact, the south-west is filling in with cloud and rain. I fly lower. Following shores and coastlines can be very deceptive. In worsening visibility, we hang on to our security: the clear distinction between water and land. But unfortunately, a deception creeps in: it's all too easy to follow the shoreline up some glen one never noticed in better visibility. The compass would certainly warn us about this move, but would we pick it up with all the buffeting?

Fort William passes in the mists and rain squalls. I slow the old airframe and wonder just where we are. I'll give Connel Bridge, Oban a call. They have an odd frequency 118*05 that can upset the run of radio frequencies all too easily to keep the *0 in the next one to be dialled up. I'm too low, but I hear something and get a glimpse of where the aerodrome should be. I fly slightly away from the coast and cling to Lismore Island, which gives a better heading to the south-west.

The coastline's like a theatre stage. It reminds me of sets I made for Jimmy Scotland's theatre productions of Shakespeare. *A Midsummer Night's Dream* in clouds. Nothing very recognisable, though the surface is still quite clear. Light and shade, side-lighting, and moving theatre dollies. Act 1, Scene 1, and the wonderful sequences at the turn of a switch. My sailing experience on Gusto is more valuable than my stage design, and I remember sailing round this area well. I'm looking for the unusual Dorus Mor, Scarba, and the Corrievrechan Whirlpool. The baleful shape of Scarba forms itself in my little theatre, and I look over to port stage left hoping to see the Crinan Hotel. The white shape of the Crinan Hotel can be seen with a hopeful clearing of the rain behind Knapdale over to Loch Fyne.

There is a wonderful heading of 130" M, which runs right down to West Kilbride on the Ayrshire Coast. Hope rises. I had wondered about staying the night at Oban, but tonight is the opening of the exhibition in Irvine, an exhibition I very much want to see.

The visibility improves, but just as I approach Prestwick, which always seems to have better visibility than round about, heavy rain strikes relentlessly. I land on runway 31 and taxi in to the flying club.

Aeroplane Seeking Gravity by James Hardie, 2009

Lost in Irvine

"Fear of flying, snakes and ladders, ancient sunlight lights the land,
textures grow and die every minute of the shortest flight"

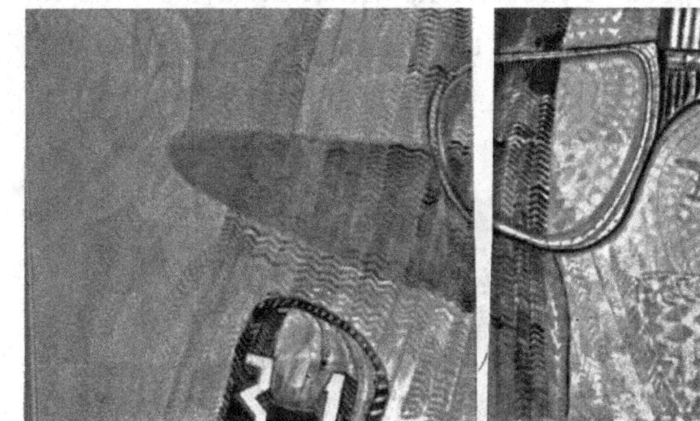
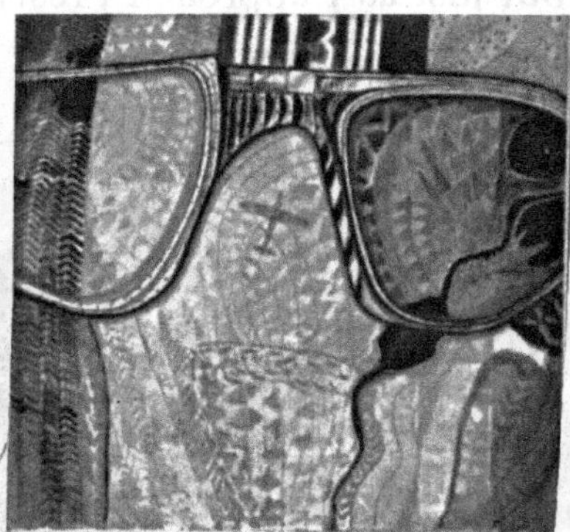
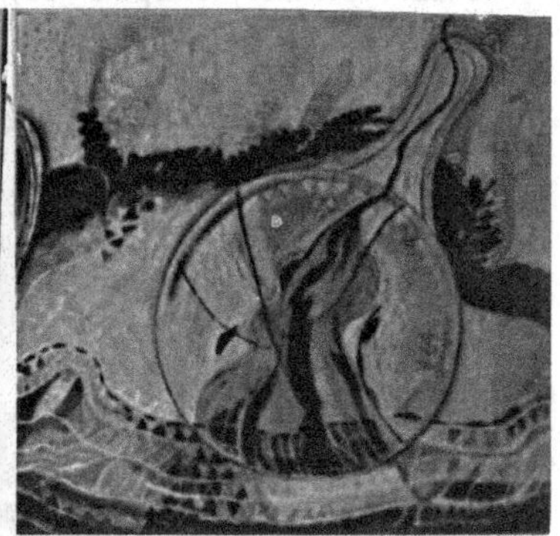

Every Minute of the Shortest Flight by James Hardie, 2009

The rain eases and I manage to open the cockpit doors of the Nord, collect my maps, headphones, kneepads, and checklists. After that, I jump down to earth. The flying club is deserted. Days of rain have dampened the comings and goings, and I sit in a large armchair very much like the end of the main feature at the cinema – it's the same kind of seat and atmosphere. My cup of tea tastes wonderful, but I have to face the window and watch the curtains of rain confuse the familiar hills and perimeters of this beautiful aerodrome. The time is 3:00 p.m. on Thursday 28 June 2007.

Tonight, at 7:00 p.m., there is an exhibition in Irvine in the Harbour Arts Centre: "A Retrospective of Alasdair Taylor." I saw Alasdair for the first time in Larkhall Academy in 1953. He was a dark-haired man who moved like a drummer and engaged everybody with his Highland accent and jumpy rhythms. He came from Coalburn and was taking his fourth, fifth, and sixth years at Larkhall Academy. Coalburn was about 12 ml. by train up on the moors and hills, and his father was the station master. Alasdair travelled by train every day.

I had discovered art in Larkhall Academy. Jim Barclay was an enthusiastic art teacher not long out of art school himself, and he treated Alasdair and I like fellow art students. All the gossip and life of the art school became familiar to us even though we had hardly seen the famous McIntosh Art School in Renfrew Street in the big city. Jim's fiancée, a post-graduate student named Margaret Horner, was a great disciple of David Donaldson A.R.S.A., whom she and Jim felt was starting a new school of painting in Glasgow.

Alasdair, two years older than I, was already thinking about leaving school. He fancied working in the whisky distillery at Edderton Ross-Shire where he was born or trying to get to Jordanhill College to become a gym teacher. He loved football. However, this picture of art that Jim Barclay painted really caught his imagination. His drawing became, for him, like playing the drums and football; his drawings contained a certain eloquence that surprised him. He read Van Gogh's letters and light began to dawn. He felt very competitive about everything and seemed jumpy and touchy in the art room. His temperament was something new in Larkhall. Larkhall Academy encouraged both of us, and I remember being in Shakespeare's *A Midsummer Night's Dream* set in the open at Morgan Glen where I was Demetrius and Alasdair was Lysander.

At the end, Mr White, the English teacher, had Alasdair and I dress up in our Shakespearean costumes and rush through the Larkhall audience of parents with drawn swords disclaiming our midsummer confusion as we searched for the lovely Helena and Hermia. We carried our confusion to Glasgow School of Art, still searching passionately for Helena and Hermia. Somehow the script was set and started with a vengeance.

As Alasdair Gray wrote in his retrospective, *Alasdair Taylor,* "Son of a stationmaster in Ross Shire and Lanarkshire, Alasdair Taylor trained at Glasgow School of Art." In his last year there, he met Annelise, a wise, practical, beautiful, Danish woman who loved art even though she was not an artist herself. They married, lived as wardens of Glasgow University Church of Scotland Chaplaincy Centre, and had two daughters. The centre closed in 1965. They moved to the lovely North Bank cottage on the Clyde shore between the clachan of Portencross and Hunterston power station, both out of sight half a mile away or more. It was rented cheaply from a local farmer because it lacked electricity and because he wished people living there to ensure the fields beside it were not robbed. The daughters grew up there. Alasdair taught evening classes in art for Glasgow University, sometimes reviewing exhibitions for BBC Radio, Scotland.

Apart from Annelise, Alasdair only loved making pictures and sculptures, so he gave up these jobs when she became a community education worker in Dalry. She died of cancer in 1994 after getting electricity with hot running water and a telephone into the cottage. Alasdair lived there until he was felled by a stroke in November 2004. His daughters supervised his nursing until his death at Greenock Central Hospital on

1 January 2007. He is buried beside Annelise in West Kilbride Graveyard under the circular, red, granite tombstone he designed.

The rain intensifies and the perimeters of Prestwick fade away. I'm going to stay in the flying club until it's time to go to the Exhibition three hours away. I still feel like I'm in limbo between flying and being. I have another cup of tea. Later that year, in a Christmas card, I learn that Jim Barclay, our famous teacher, died that very afternoon in 2007.

When it's time to go, I lock the flying club behind me and drive away. Irvine always confuses me, especially when I approach from the south instead of the north. I pick a road and meander towards the town centre. The River Irvine is clear from the sky, but it complicates the roads and entry to the harbour round giant supermarkets and garish town centres. I get lost. I stop awkwardly and wind the window down. Two young men look at me damply. "How do I get to the Harbour Arts Centre?" I ask. They are obviously disgusted with me in my big car. "You're *gawn* the *wrang* way – entirely, by the way." He leans aggressively into the car and talks to me as if I were 5 years old. I still feel like I'm flying down the Great Glen, and my confusion stems from that flight in part. "Turn left, and then left again and straight on at the roundabout." I am in a trance as I contemplate rain and bright lights and no shape to anything through the misty windscreens. I start to move off, but I'm halted by the guy's words: "For fuck's sake, *yer wrang* again. Jesus Christ. See that bus? Follow the fucking bus; *sharely* you can *dae* that at least!" He's quite right: my direction-finding is used up.

I found my own Helena, like Alasdair's Annelise. Her name was Ann Livingston. I met her, too, at Glasgow School of Art. She was *A Midsummer Night's Dream* beautiful, and like Alasdair and Annelise, we got married and had two daughters. We lived in Fife. I remember travelling to the Edinburgh Festival in about 1962. Life as an art teacher was strangely tense – it was as though something was just around the corner but just out of reach.

We would go to the Festival Fringe. We would recharge our batteries. The University Of South California Academy Of Performing Arts was just what the doctor ordered. The play was Edward Albee's *Zoo Story.* We had seen his famous *"Who's afraid of Virginia Woolf".* It was so new! How could two characters on a park bench reach such intensity? I was transfixed. My wife fades from my side as I live the passionate business of dramatic art. How strange this weakness is. I've always felt the artist is in a majority of one.

First of all, the character is dominating. He is triumphant as he probes and reveals. This revelation, this slight secret is grabbed by the other character, and – my god! – What a change takes place. We watch as these humans change places and achieve superiority and lose it. I'm astonished. That's what it's all about. That's what we should be aware of. I want to rush back to my studio and paint *Zoo Stories.*

We drive back to Fife. It's a beautiful September night, and we stop for a late supper at the Queensferry Inn at the Ferry. We have peppered fillet steaks (my very first time I've such a cut). We glow and the world glows back.

The Day before

Back at Inverness Airport, Graham collects the mini-DV tapes from the camera in the Nord. We've filmed for four hours. The evening hushes and darkens. The Moray coast has a strong quality one always notices – it's energetic and sinewy.

Graham and Kevin haven't been wearing headphones and are deafened by the six cylinders of the inverted French engine, but Graham drives us back to Garmouth where we meet his wife, Addie, and their beautiful baby.

Will the film work? I wonder. Every trial has been a failure with the vertical camera, but we have two other HD digital cameras in the aircraft. We watch anxiously as the discs are fed into the computer and we hold our breath as the vertical camera pulses along the coast and river like an eye in the sky. I've never seen anything like it. It's wonderful. The vertical camera and the angled camera combine through the aircraft's track to provide some rhythm to the beat of the harbours and landscape. I hope Telford can see it.

I stumble to bed that night totally exhausted but not lost. I can only think about flying.

Flying

Transcription of an interview. Sandy Moffat, head of painting studios Glasgow School of Art. 167 Renfrew Street, Glasgow. June 1993.

Sandy Moffat is sitting in his seat against the background of his McIntosh studio. He says the following:

"Flying is one of the big subjects in art. It has been for a long, long time. The Greeks, of course, had their gods flying – Icarus flew, Pegasus flew. And not just Western cultures … all cultures and religions have paintings, drawings of creatures flying in the heavens, up there. Up there in the sky there must be thousands of wonderful paintings of angels in Western art.

"Flying in the age of reason, say, towards the late eighteenth century, I think really preoccupied the minds of many thinking people. Goya, for example, shows this in his paintings of hot-air balloons. There are lots of flying people in Goya's paintings, lots of thoughts about flight. How could man fly? How could we make a machine to take us up in the air, make a machine to storm the heavens and challenge God."

"Of course, it wasn't until the early twentieth century that the aeroplane was invented, built, and made to fly. A very important symbol for artists was Bleriot's crossing of the Channel. It was celebrated in paintings by Delaunay and inspired poems by Rilke, Apollinaire, and writers of the time. The advent of the pilot and the aeroplane became a model of modernity.

"Then, of course, the advent of the First World War rapid improvements were made and this was even more a symbol of modernity. There was the pioneering abstract painting of flight and aircraft by Malevich based on patterns of aircraft in the sky. The Italian Futurists published an Aero Pittura Manifesto and decided to paint aeroplane pictures. They gave the aeroplane a central role in their art. The aeroplane was seen as very romantic. I don't think it was until the late thirties that there was a change, when the aeroplane became a byword for murderous efficiency. The Spanish Civil

War-Guernica the murderous efficiency of the bomber squadron; artists' thinking changed ... it became problematic, thinking changed at this time."

"The whole idea of flying in this cockpit, this little cockpit surrounded by the immensity of space; above, below and beyond. It is a remarkable, unique way of seeing that is now available to us in the twentieth century. We had imagined it; artists had dreamed of flying. Primitive religions tried to depict flying – some images of flight on wall paintings or sculptures – images have always been there. Now we can do it and see it for ourselves. Jim Hardie has flown all over Scotland and other places for a quarter century. He's in a unique position as a painter and a pilot. He's been making pretty unique things for this quarter century. In fact, I envy Jim being able to fly a plane.

* * *

In 2000, Pam and I went on a search. We went to Toledo in Spain to see a painting that I think is the first flying masterpiece. The painting is in Toledo Cathedral, and we travelled down to the Tajo on a bus. El Greco is the artist, and the painting is "Burial of Count Orgaz," his masterpiece. I first saw the painting in 1966. Still in Fife, I had bought a large house, "Largo Lea," which had always been used as a boarding house. To pay the rates, we kept it a boarding house in the summer and let it out completely. This allowed us to go off on our travels.

What was round the corner? We wondered. We had a tent and camped all over France and Spain. We camped at Toledo and were taken up by the amazing family of Thomas Bernal of The Calle Olvido, Madrid. My sister, Vera, who was travelling with us, was going to stay a year with the family as an au pair girl. Spanish hospitality was lavish, but before moving to Madrid, I explored Toledo. I painted every day, finding so many images and motifs in this Moorish–Christian frontier. But El Greco's "Burial of Count Orgaz" was the first time I felt the force of man depicting the gods. They were flying creatures. Flying creatures in the seventeenth century, in the age of reason. Flying; flying; flying!

Back in Scotland, I heard about a mysterious airplane builder somewhere down my way in Ayrshire. A technician at Glasgow School of Art, Jim Lambert, mentioned that somebody was building aeroplanes on the Isle of Bute. Jim's model aeroplane magazine had mentioned that there was someone in Rothesay who had a real, full-sized Tiger Moth in his living room!

I live just across the water from Rothesay on the Isle of Bute, so I phoned the police and inquired. "His name's Tom Crawford, and he has got one flying, one in his garage, and yes, there's a Tiger Moth in his living room. Here's his phone number."

Tom's story was the stuff of legend. He had served as a pilot in the RAF in the Second World War, and when he returned he had emigrated to Canada to start a boatyard! He became a professional boat builder. After twenty years of this, he returned to Britain – not to Scotland, but to Northern Ireland and became a manager at Shorts Aeroplane Co. in Belfast. He was constructing aeroplanes there!

In the thirties, he had met my naked pilots, Amy Johnson and Jim Mollison. He found Amy very interested in his talk of streamlining. In those days, the pilots thought of more power - more speed, but Tom's experience of gliders showed that if one could cut down drag, one could improve performance.

"If the aeroplane can go through the air easier, stands to reason you will get more speed for the same power setting in your Gypsy Moth. Streamline where the wings attach to the fuselage and clean up everything that causes drag," Tom Crawford was a terrific example of bringing the aeroplane home. Literally he brought three light aeroplanes into his home at Port Bannatyne. His life, his style took all this so naturally in its stride. I remember trying to find his house during that first visit. I was riding my old motorbike and sidecar, and after a few turns, I came upon a hillside cottage covered with fallen leaves. Tom emerged from his garage, spanner in hand, not too pleased at being interrupted. Flying seemed so natural in this setting - of hands on making the flying machine; it was no surprise to learn how Tom started flying. He said, "I learned to fly myself, of course, I built my own glider and was catapulted off the Campsie Fells. If the wing dropped, you picked it up; I used to do the same thing when I built models: made the correction, picked the wing up, corrected the altitude of the nose, and transferred these thoughts to bigger aeroplanes." I asked, "You've been building aeroplanes all your life?" Tom answered "Since I was 8 years old, they just got bigger and bigger, that was all." And "I believe you met Amy Johnson and her husband, Jim Mollison." Tom responded "I talked to her mainly about drag. She was flying in the Kings Cup Air Race, and most of the aircraft she was flying against were similar aircraft, and most powered planes in those days were only interested in horsepower, not interested in cutting down the drag in streamlining for more speed the way they are today. With my background of sailplanes and gliders, we streamlined where the wings met fuselage and various struts and tailplanes. She could add 5 mph easily for the same throttle settings, so she did that." I then asked, "What aeroplane did Amy have? Tom continues "I think this was Jason 4, a Gypsy 3 A." I wanted to know more "How did Amy take this advice?" And Tom answered "She thought that was great – "I never given much thought to this, she said, 'but if it goes through the air easier without adding power, it must gain speed.'"

Tom then noted, "We've got today sailplanes, and power aircraft have got to watch out for them. They're overtaking them, and that's without an engine. I met Jim Mollison at Renfrew when he came back from the Cape. Cape Town to London in a Puss Moth in eight hours." I asked, did he have any special equipment? "Oh no! explained Tom, just the standard, just the usual. At Renfrew, we pushed his Puss Moth into the hangar, and I happened to notice that his pitot head was corroded, so I broke it off. I told him to get another one. In fact, I've got the old one back here after all these years." I queried, "Jim Mollison was from Glasgow?" "Bearsden." "That flight across the Atlantic crash-landed at Bridgeport, just 37 ml. short of New York. Jim was ill for a long time. Amy wasn't so badly hurt. In fact, I don't think he ever got over it." "Do you think it put them off?" Tom answered, "It didn't put anybody off. In fact, you're imbued with the idea of flying, there's only one thing that'll put you off – that's when it'll put you off completely."

Propellers and Parachutes

Stories and flying; flying and stories. How do people see flying? I remember leaving Tom Crawford and Port Bannatyne determined that I would not just be another story, that I would take his advice and rebuild this old aeroplane and make it into a flying machine. Every night once the fuselage was installed in my hangar/garage (with the tail sticking out), I lay in bed dreaming of the big take off and advancing the throttle. Pam was not amused.

My first film, *Aeroplane for the Naked Pilot,* documents the travels of the original fuselage, complete with engine, from Prestwick to Skelmorlie, from Skelmorlie to Glasgow, from Glasgow to Skelmorlie, from Skelmorlie to Perth, from Perth to Edinburgh, from Edinburgh to Prestwick. We paused at the Collins Gallery in Glasgow where the aeroplane was exhibited in a marquee tent complete with a soundtrack of the engine. Without its wings, it looked potent but bound to the earth. I knew I was going to need a lot of help.

The newspaper headlines were peculiar:

Nazi Plane Built in Skelmorlie
"Is it going anywhere near Clydebank?"
Greenock Herald

"Flying High, the Man Who Built a Messerschmitt Fighter Plane
in His Garden Shed (and Didn't Tell the Neighbours)"

Daily Mail
"Propellers and Parachutes as Flying Goes Back to Basics"
Spectator (Northern Ireland)
Iain Gray

The last article is by far the best. Iain Gray actually flew in the Nord and tells his story with talent and insight: "A low-flying Luftwaffe fighter was seen over the skies of Newtonards last week. Rather than a crew of war-like Nazis, however, the Messerschmitt contained the marginally more friendly face of an intrepid *Spectator* journalist.

"The aircraft, a ME 108 painstakingly restored to a World War Two look by owner Jim Hardie was of course over for the Ulster Air Show at the weekend. Last Friday (22nd) however, I was privileged enough to be given a brief airborne tour of the peninsula in the machine. It was, it has to be said, very different to my usual experience of flight on modern-day passenger aircraft. There were no stewardesses offering boiled sweets for a start, and complimentary drinks were decidedly lacking.

On the plus side, there were no screaming babies, though this was more than made up for by the noise of the flight. With no insulation or double glazing and pilot Declan Curtis understandably wearing the only helmet, the main feature of the jaunt that springs to mind is the sheer volume. The only thing capable of drowning out the high pitched whoosh of the wind was the low busy roar of the engine, with the latter also providing the only source of heat for the Messerschmitt occupants.

Slightly worrying for myself was that Declan was also wearing the only parachute, whereas I was clad in a three-piece suit. More stylish, perhaps, but not much use above ground level. I was nonetheless reassured when Jim informed me that the plane had fully passed all of the myriad safety examinations required by current aviation authorities.

"Such low-tech surroundings really emphasize just how cosseted contemporary flyers are compared to their 1940s counterparts. Although I was still a very long way from the plush chairs and in-flight entertainment of the average Boeing. In many ways it was an improvement, though, even though I only experienced a short, half-hour jaunt involving a couple of loops around Strangford Lough and a quick zoom over the hamlets and villages of the peninsula. The Messerschmitt never got above 2,000.

"It also felt more like real flying, if you see what I mean. Large passenger aircraft are these days closer to a living room than a vehicle, whereas the ME 108 with its utilitarian interior door opened by rope and strictly functional, pared down design is a much more raw and thrilling encounter. After we landed, Jim explained that I had travelled in comparative luxury. The leather rear double seat of the Messerschmitt was favoured by the top German brass, thus apparently putting me on a level with Herman Goering … sadly not the first time such a parallel has been drawn.

"He told me exactly how he had become one of the very few men to own such a craft and almost certainly the only artist to spend nearly fifteen years of his life restoring a Luftwaffe fighter to working order.

"Jim is an amateur flier at home in Scotland but found the ME 108 when scouting material for a Glasgow Art exhibition in 1993. It was abandoned in a field in Prestwick – little more than a husk with grass growing through it, but its potential shone past the grime and years of neglect. 'It was perfect for the exhibition, which was called '*The Naked Pilot*' he reminisced, 'but in order to move it, I had to put on an alternative undercarriage. During the process, I got fascinated by the engineering, the craftsmanship, and puzzle solving that goes into fabricating new parts for such a plane, and that was really the beginning of the whole process.'

"It was at this time that Jim discovered a second use for Messerschmitts: terrifying employees of twenty-four-hour petrol stations. 'After the exhibition, we were towing it through Glasgow on a dirty, wet night,' he laughed. 'The chap who was pulling it behind his Land Rover told me he had to get petrol, so we pulled into this garage forecourt, plane and all, while it's teeming with rain. I couldn't resist it; I went up to the girl behind the counter and asked for 200 gallons for my ME 108. She screamed her head off. She actually thought I had landed on the road and was threatening to call the police, but its strange things like that which have made owning it a delight.'

Parts

At first Jim was resigned to leaving the Messerschmitt unrepaired, having heard local engineers complaining that it is impossible even to renovate more common or more recent light aircraft due to the short shelf life of spare parts. A chance encounter with a French journalist led to the discovery that these planes are regarded as classics on the European mainland, however, and he was soon able to contact a dealer in Paris who could supply him with the necessary equipment. 'It's not like a vintage car, these parts are almost impossible to find,' continued Jim, 'so I wound up meeting this guy who turned out to be madder than me. He hates the English and refuses to speak their language, but fortunately, I know a passing amount of French. Because I'm Scottish, he assumed I lived in a tower and supported the Jacobite rebellion. So he was more than happy to sell me the parts at a very good price.

"'I assembled the whole thing in my home, taking up an entire large bedroom for many years, but looking back on it; it has not been a great hassle to me. In many ways, it was a trial-and-error process, actually a lot like painting, and I think that kind of lateral thinking helped. Looking back, I have forgotten the struggle, the times when nothing worked, and now it is just so satisfying to fly.'

"Jim described his restoration project as a labour of love, though he admits other people tend to reach a different verdict. 'They say I must be obsessed,' he joked, "but to me it was an art project. Using an aeroplane in my mind is really no different to using a palette and brushes. In fact, that is how I got my start in flying a long time ago. I was a typical starving artist, but I paid for my flying lessons by painting the tails of aeroplanes. Occasionally, an opportunity comes your way that you know you have to grab with both hands. Only in my wildest dreams did I think I would ever own my own plane, but now here we are. It just goes to show that a silly dreamer can get things done, even in aviation, which is the most severely regulated field you will ever get.'

"He also plans to involve the plane in his craft in a practical level and has fitted a camera in anticipation of a forthcoming event in the north of Scotland that will see him and other artists use the *ME 108* to photograph landscapes in the Highlands.

Tribute

Jim is careful to pay tribute to Declan without whose dedication and expertise the owner insists the Messerschmitt would be almost impossible to fly. The two hooked up through mutual acquaintances on the vintage circuit where Declan, by trade a commercial airline pilot, fulfils his lifelong dreams by performing as a display flyer in his spare time.

"Declan explained he was first inspired to fly as a boy growing up in a council estate in Dublin where, as he puts it, residents had not paid for their houses so could not object to the noise from a nearby airport. 'There were always planes going overhead,' he remembers, 'and that combined with old Second World War films on TV really seared aviation into my brain. I started off fuelling planes then working as a mechanic at a local flying club before eventually becoming an engineer with big airlines in London. Even then, though, I was volunteering to work on Spitfires at the Imperial War Museum. In the end, I decided to leave the mechanical side of it altogether and retrained as a commercial pilot. It's a great job, but I was always interested in the classical planes.'

"Declan owns a De Havilland Chipmunk, a training aircraft used during World War Two and got into display flying through attending vintage aviation fairs. He was merely there to show his plane on Static parks, but he was encouraged by the display airmen to get it airborne. "All these guys flying Spitfires or Hurricanes have a delightful soft spot for the Chipmunk. They all think it's a great plane and told me I had to fly it. So in the end, up I went,' he continued. 'You have to remember that this kind of flying is all about the spirit behind it. Why do you want to be a display pilot, to show off? No, wrong. It has to be to display the aircraft in a gentle manner so that the audience can see its best assets. After a great deal of training, I can now display a large range of aeroplanes down to as low as 50 ft, but there are always limitations, and it is a very controlled environment. It is very disciplined, which is one of the reasons why I love it. But all that meant when I got together with Jim I was used to dealing with very similar technology, and with the right information, it was relatively simple to get to grips with the ME 108.'

"The big question, of course, is how Declan thinks the four-seater, single-propeller Messerschmitt compares to the enormous passenger jet planes he pilots in his day job. 'These days, airliners are very much driven by automatics,' he says, 'the cockpit is like a TV screen, and in many ways, it is similar to a PlayStation your kids would have. Although it is a very busy environment, actually flying the aircraft is a relatively light workload; it is only take off and landing where you have to handle the plane, but because it is so modern, everything is very stable.' This could not be in stronger contrast to the ME 108 designed in the thirties when much of aviation was in its infancy and most of the systems today's pilots rely on were not even on the drawing board. 'There are a lot of features on the Messerschmitt that are not on modern aircraft,' added Declan, 'and the reason they aren't there is because they didn't work. They are beautiful pieces of machinery, but they can be difficult. It is not overcomplicated to fly, but one has to keep one's eye on the ball, and safety precautions are, of course, paramount. It is a joy to pilot, though, and in doing this, I am basically combining my hobby with my profession. For that, I am very grateful to Jim for allowing me a chance to fly the *ME 108*. I love it, what more can I say?'"

Ruchenlage

Ruchenlage is German for *upside down,* and in April 2007, my ideas about art and aeroplanes were going to be turned upside down. My daughter, Amy Hardie, worked in Edinburgh College of Art where she was a head of research and development in film and videotape. She has her own documentary film company, Docspace, and she has been having adventures with documentary films for twenty years. She told me about the Scottish Documentary Institute who put up money for a series of short documentary films on the theme of lies. Somebody was looking for a Messerschmitt.

Amy introduced me to a dynamic duo: Astrid Bussink and Sonja Henrici. Astrid had become famous due to a documentary, *Angel Makers,* which presents the story of poisoning. She won a Newcomers Award. She was from the Netherlands and hardly said a word, so Sonja arranged everything and gave out the money. Ruchenlage was going to be the story of Rudolf Hess's flight to Scotland in a Messerschmitt on 10 May 1941.

Astrid, Sonja, Ian Dodd (the cameraman), and a parachute arrived at Prestwick Airport.

"There was a grandiose loneliness over the North Sea." [14]

"At 10:00 p.m. I crossed Scotland's east coast near Holy Island."

"I flew so low over a small village."

"You had to turn the plane upside down and let yourself fall out of it." "How to jump out of a plane."

"I began to turn it over and shot downwards in a curve."

"The plane's gigantic centrifugal force kept us trapped inside."

"I was upside down, and all the blood was spun out of my head." "Before my eyes, I saw the dreaded bomber pilots' stars." I thought *I'm just above the ground flying straight down; I'm going to crash. Could this be the end?* "Then it all went black and I lost consciousness." "Everything was circling around me, but then I finally came to … like Adam awakening to the consciousness of the world on his first day." "I had no idea where I was or what had happened to me." "Slowly, I realised that I had arrived at my destination."

I found this list so evocative, and painting gave me so many metaphors for similar experiences. On 9 September 2008 at 2,000 feet above Oban, my engine erupted into a terrible vibration. The real thing, the real here and now. I thought I should maintain height at 70 knots. I said, "Oban Radio G MD, I have a technical problem. Immediate return to the field and request immediate landing runway 1." Back comes the quick reply, "G- MD understand technical problem. Clear for immediate landing. No traffic."

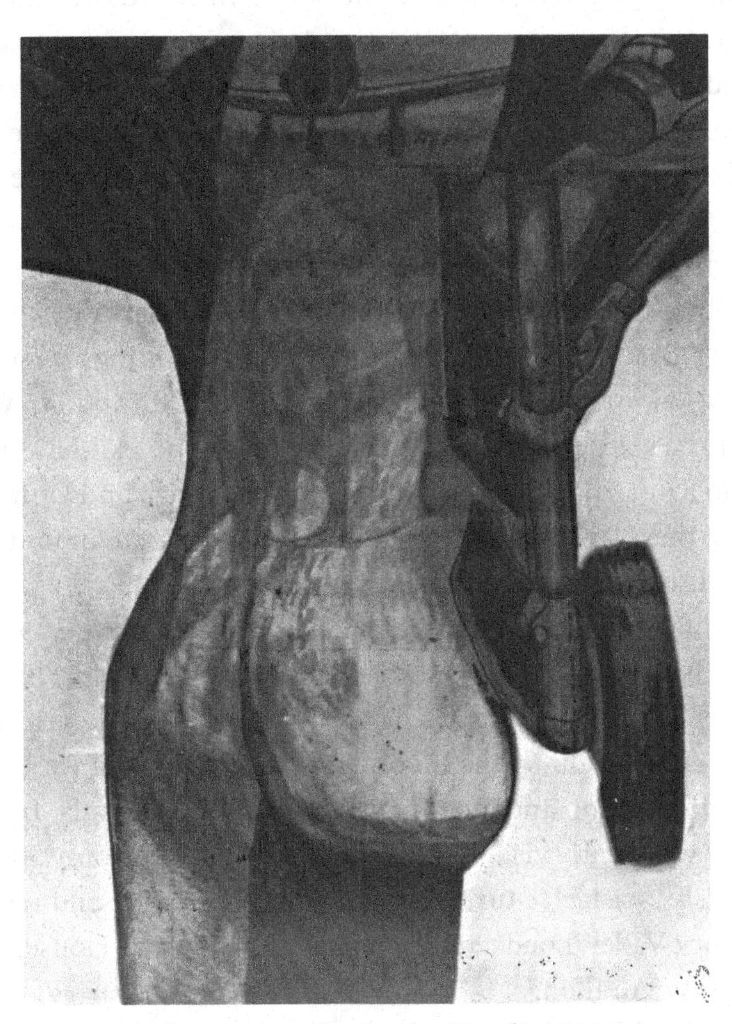

Undercarriage by James Hardie, 1996

Beside me is Robert Howie from Skelmorlie. Robert, a friend of my stepson, David, had his first flight with me when he was 12. "This is good, Jim, you concentrate on the field and landing, and I'll watch the dials," says Robert. Robert is now a highly qualified commercial pilot. Could the vibration be the undercarriage – a very early, retracting, and tricycle undercarriage. Should I try it down to see if I get the three greens? If the engine stops, where will I land? I will land directly below if I don't have any power."

Robert and I go over the procedures. We make the field before flaps or undercarriage go down and we aim for one-third of the way down in case the propeller stops on finals. We are over the sea and about 3 mi from touchdown, maintaining height. There is another runway, which is closed, but it's nearer and it's an option if the engine seizes finally.

This moment of truth takes me back to filmmaking. A build-up to a climax: the moment of truth. "I began to turn it over and shot downwards in a curve." *Could this be the end?* It's an interesting moment – the point of no return so beloved by the human psyche. The build-up is everything. I loved working with the filmmakers, especially during the research phase. Rudolf Hess's flight is the most notorious use of an aeroplane that doesn't include destruction that there is. "There was a grandiose loneliness over the North Sea."

Two students from Glasgow University, Sigi Cassel and Ian Shearman, came down to Prestwick, and we tried to retrace Hess's Flight from Dungavel Reservoir to Ailsa Craig and back to Dugavel House. Sigi was interested in painting and photography and sought to produce black and white photographs for Aerolab, and Ian was a computer expert who would be able to string our ideas together for an exhibition piece. We flew from Prestwick to Kilmarnock; saw Louden Hill, Strathaven, and Dungavel Reservoir. We could imagine these large reservoirs standing out on a clear, moonlit night in 1941.

We had read Hess's letters to his wife, written in Spandau Prison, Berlin, where he was to spend his life after his epic flight. He had navigated across the North Sea and sped towards the British coast to avoid interception by the RAF. Flying very low, he had navigated by conspicuous hills, lochs, and reservoirs, and eventually found the *L*-shaped Dungavel Reservoir in the moonlight. He had turned west for the Atlantic coast to confirm his position and identified Troon on its peninsula. In the moonlight, Paddy's Milestone was clearly visible. In his words, it was "[t]he only 500 m rock off the South West Scottish Coast." He turned back from the Atlantic and retraced his flight past Troon, Garnock Valley, Louden Hill, and back to Dungavel House, where he hoped to meet the Duke of Hamilton.

Hess hadn't been able to ask about bailing out of his Messerschmitt – he had to keep it secret – so there he was in the dark, trying to work out how to abandon his aircraft (which was probably tooling along at 300 knots). He did very well: he landed by parachute about 10 mi from Dungavel at Floors Farm, near Eaglesham.

I managed to land as well and state, "G-MD, turning on final runway one" "MD clear to land runway one. Wind 18 knots at 110 degrees."

The engine is still developing power – that takes care of the sink. The wind is slightly from the tail, but we land smoothly on the runway and the fire brigade runs along behind us. "Do you want to come to a stop on the runway?" asks Oban.

Though there is some smoke, I don't think we are on fire so I turn off the runway and ask for holding point bravo. There is great relief as we switch off and get out of MD. The connecting rod on number five cylinder has broken, allowing the piston to hit the cylinder head. All we can see is a spark plug hanging loose on its HT lead over the carburettor! Lucky!

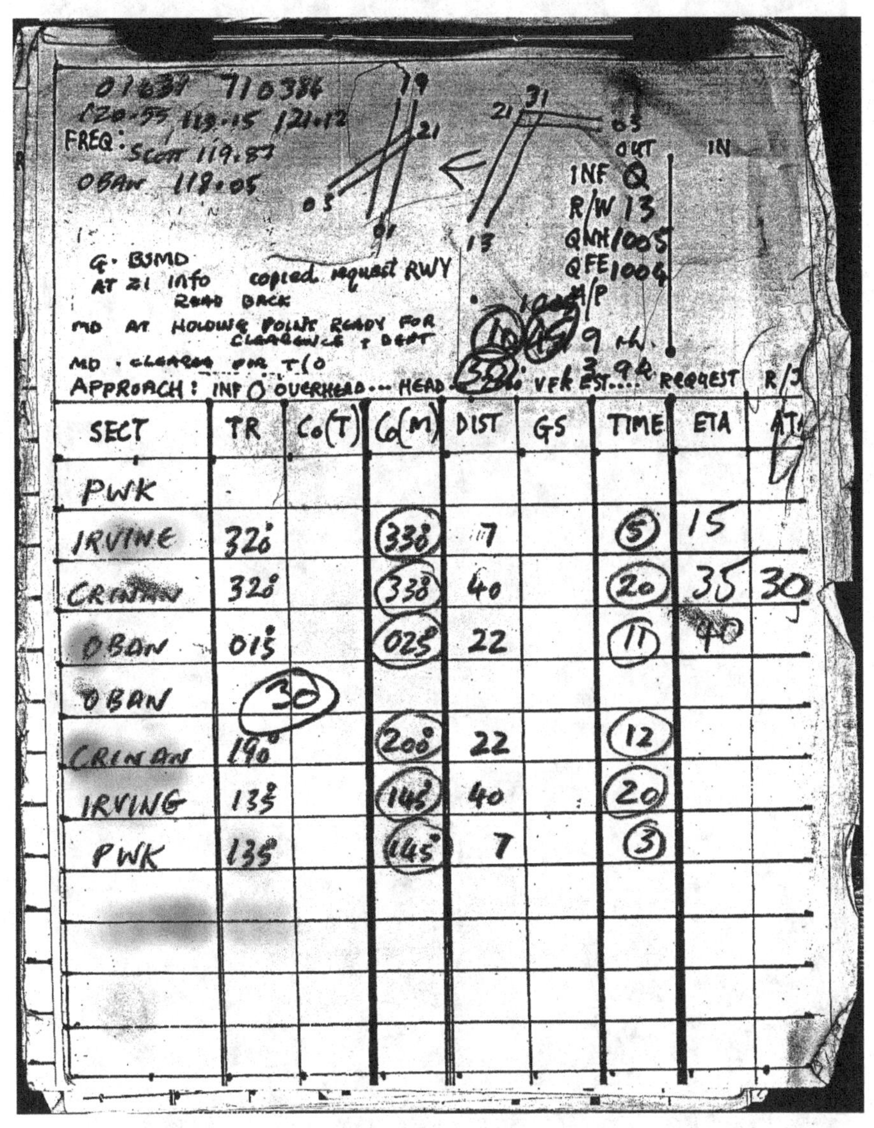

FREQ: SCOTT 119.87
OBAN 118.05

G-BSMD
AT 21 info copied. request RWY
READ BACK
MD AT HOLDING POINT READY FOR CLEARANCE & DEPT
MD CLEARED FOR T/O
APPROACH: INF O OVERHEAD... HEAD... VFR EST... REQUEST R/3

OUT IN
INF Q
R/W 13
QNH 1005
QFE 1004

SECT	TR	Co(T)	Co(M)	DIST	GS	TIME	ETA	ATA
PWK								
IRVINE	320°		338	7		5	15	
CRINAN	320°		338	40		20	35	30
OBAN	015°		025	22		11	40	
OBAN		30						
CRINAN	190°		208	22		12		
IRVING	135°		143	40		20		
PWK	135°		145°	7		3		

Flight log on a knee pad. Forced Landing North Connel 09/09/08. "How to jump out of a plane."

"I began to turn it over and shot downwards in a curve"; "the plane's gigantic centrifugal force kept me trapped inside." [14]

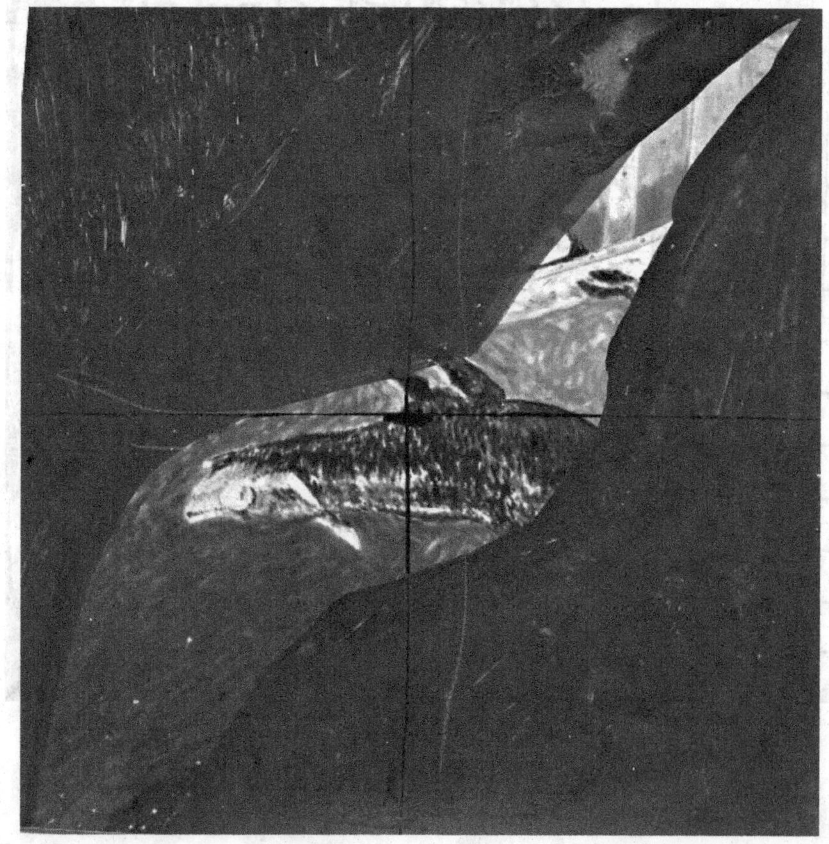

"I was upside down and all the blood was spun out of my head";
"before my eyes I saw the dreaded bomber pilots' stars."

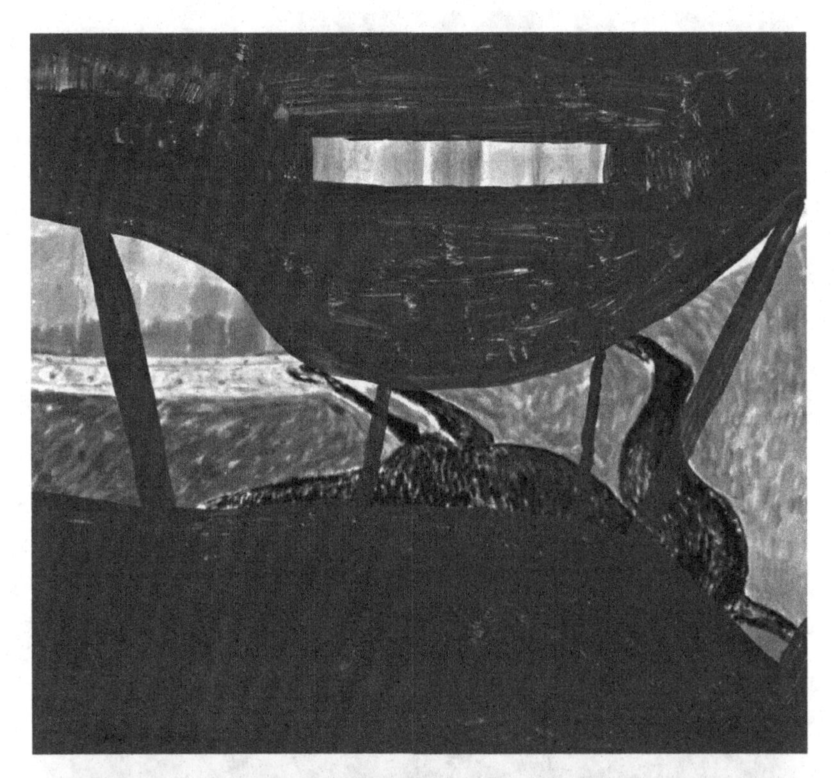

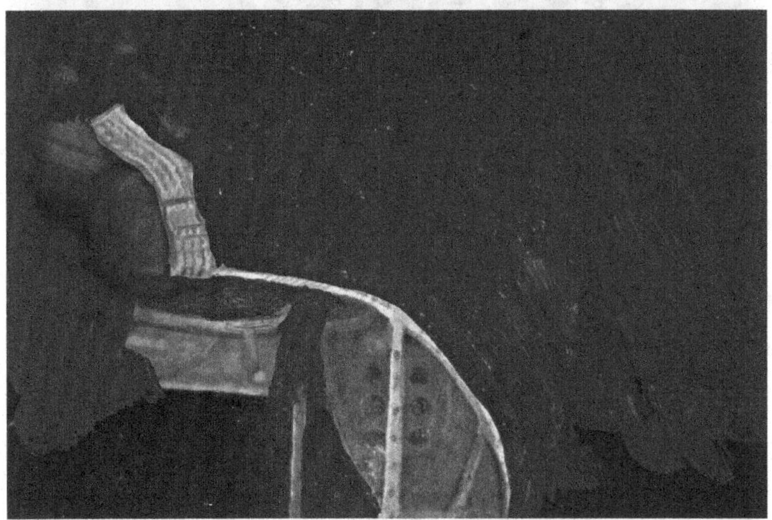

I thought *I'm just above the ground flying straight down; I'm going to crash. Could this be the end?*

"Then it all went black and I lost consciousness."

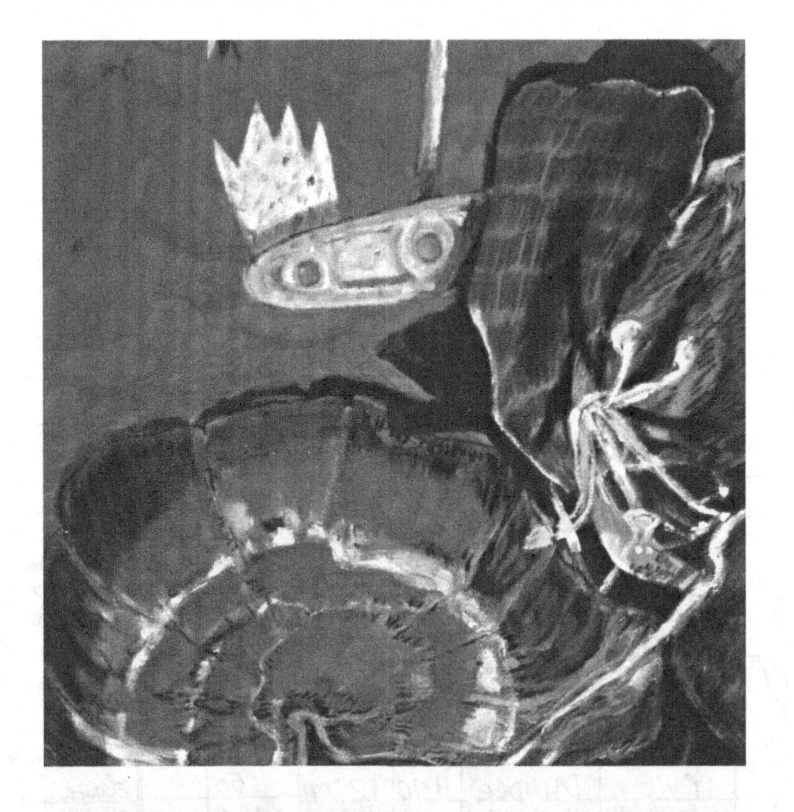

CAPTAIN	Holder's Operating Capacity	JOURNEY or Nature of Flight: From	JOURNEY or Nature of Flight: To	Departure (G.M.T.)	Arrival (G.M.T.)	(1) Single-Engine In Command	(2) Single-Engine Dual or P.2	REMARKS Including counter-signature for P.1/S
					Hrs. / Mins. Totals Brought Forward	385 ·40	116 ·10	
HARDIE	P1	local		1308	1348	:45		local Copland Barclay.
HARDIE	P1	circuits		1314	1344	:30		STOP+GO - G. MCNAUGHTON
HARDIE	P1	PWK	GLENFORSA	1710	1815	1:08		Met Amy + Peter 3 approaches
HARDIE	P1	GLENFORSA	PWK	1942	20:27	:45		Diff T. OFF not much wind.
HARDIE	P1	local		1715	17·55	:40		Skelmorlie + Bute
HARDIE	P1	PWK	DUNDEE	11·10	12:00	:50		Leuchars + St. Andrews
HARDIE	P1	DUNDEE	PWK	14.12	15:20	1:08		Memorial Flight to Dad
HARDIE	P1	Circuits .		09·57	10·35	:40		+ Geo. McNaughton (2)
HARDIE.	P1	local	PWK	15:47	16:27	:40		+ H. Copeland / Skelmorlie
CURTIS	P2	PWK	LEUCHARS	09:04	10:47	~~:45~~	:45	Leuchars Air Display
HARDIE	P1	LEUCHARS	PWK	11·30	12:21	:51		" " "
Passenger Flying 5 4 0 hours 44 minutes					Hrs. / Mins. Totals Carried Forward	393 :34	116 ·55	

Every pilot has to have a log book. All the sins are kept; all the highs and lows are put down in bare, simple facts. In 2006, I began flying with the Caledonian Chipmunks: Declan Curtis, David Friel, Martin Ruddy, and Duncan McDonald. I loved the experience of flying with commercial pilots who had logged something like 6,000 hours compared to the few hundred I had put together in thirty-seven years of flying. On 12, May 2006, the Caledonian Chipmunks and their Messerschmitt friend were bound for Perth for the weekend.

Display flying is carefully regulated – every season, the particular displays must be practised regularly and shown to an assessor. My old Nord has severe limitations when it comes to aerobatics. Most of the fuselage is held by two large doors that leave very little joining the engine and the tail. When flying it, one is not supposed to exceed three Gs.

The Chipmunks take off and we wait at Prestwick to give them a fair lead before heading out to catch them as they near Perth. The weather is fine at first, but as we head north, rain encroaches on us. Perth is 397 ft asl, and that is a big factor when flying. Therefore, given the higher ground, the two chipmunks are diverted to Dundee. Declan and I get a good sighting of the field with a 400-ft separation from the low clouds. We carried out a downwind join for runway 23 and landed in the heavy showers.

My sister, Vera, was waiting in the rain for her first sight of the elusive aeroplane that her brother talked about but never produced. She and her husband, Tober, are the first in the family to climb aboard, close the cockpit doors, and realise what *per ardua ad astra* means.

When considering my aeroplane, I'm reminded of "Figure with Unicycle" or Alan Fletcher's "Figure with Ladder." It's the connection that counts.

During the flight back on Sunday, I'm pilot-in-command. The Nord is not a dual-control aircraft; there is only one throttle and one set of brake pedals. The starboard side has the electrics, which are quite difficult to reach when flying solo. It's designed as a two-crew aircraft, which makes it quite different from modern aircraft. My confidence is building up, though, and I see the dimensions of flying open up.

The aeroplane has been so significant this century. Its connections have blown away the art dreams of El Greco and the Italian Futurists. It has become a weapon of mass destruction, a polluter of the planet, a tool used for commercial exploitation, and the prison that keeps people anxiously circling the globe like migrating birds. My experience has led me to use the aeroplane as art to kick-start art. But this is the wonderful thing about humanity: we must measure ourselves against our experience ... and the texture and colour know no bounds.

Log Book (RAF Leuchars Air Show)

My father died in 2006, two months after Perth. He lived in St Andrews and had been in the RAF during the war. I decide to try a memorial flight. Planning a flight like this elucidates the holes in my experience in terms of dealing with air traffic and permissions for such a trip.

I talk to Dundee and RAF Leuchars and explain what I'd like to do. The plan is to fly to Dundee where the air traffic controllers will contact RAF Leuchars to arrange what we want to do with all the other movements of a busy fighter command station. Declan brings his two boys in their flying suits. E'oin and Osin are convinced somebody's going to shoot at them while flying in such an aeroplane, but they're ready for anything.

On a beautiful, clear day in August, we touch down at Dundee. I'm trying long, careful approaches at this time, still wary of the sink and the lack of braking from the thirties-style, original brakes. The brakes are fine for taxiing, but they fade if used in the landing. Speed is everything, and at 55 knots the Nord lands after about 800 m without braking.

We talk about my father and that generation of the Second World War to the young controllers in Dundee and Leuchars. Nearly everybody we meet had relatives in the forces. Connections don't last, but they are interesting.

Leuchars allows us to fly right over the centre of the RAF base at 1,000 ft and fly round the town of St Andrews about 1 mi away. For me, the connections have a fragility and delicacy not typically associated with an old aeroplane's noise and racket. The controls on these old, vintage aeroplanes have a different feel than modern aeroplanes. We take three orbits around St Andrews. My mother and sister see us flying down the "Chariots of Fire" beach and manage to get back to the family home on the outskirts of St Andrews. The whole Sunday morning is stopped in time, and there seems to be no noise left. As we fly past Fife Ness and up the Forth, we can see the mountains of Arran across Scotland, and the flight home to Prestwick completes the composition.

A few weeks later, we are on display at Leuchars itself. I remember Leuchars well from the fifties. In 1954 I was a schoolboy in the Royal Observer Corps. I was part of the Battle of Britain Day display. The displays were breathtaking Tiger Moths, Spitfires, Hunters, and Swifts. Books brought out at this time were dazzling. I remember asking for Pierre Closterman's *The Big Show* in 1953. Closterman, born in Brazil, had a degree in aeronautical engineering. He presented himself to the RAF in 1940 at the age of 19. He was an exceptionally talented writer, artist, and fighter pilot. He had a great respect for his German adversaries, and much of his book was censored in 1953. It was only recently that the rest of his book was reinserted into the original text.

On that day in 1954, I looked over a Boulton Paul Balliol trainer. The sergeant pilot flying instructor was just setting out to return to RAF Valley after a long day on display, but he still had the patience to make his job real to us on the ground. He was looking forward to his tea, but after listening to him, I felt I could be a pilot, too.

Much later, in 2006, the boys are doing formation aerobatics. For my first year, I'm a static display. Next year, we'll be displaying the Nord. We set off from Prestwick and join up near Leuchars. In formation, we approach Leuchars and the three aircraft break for a one-after-another landing. It was amazing!

This is the first time I've flown into an RAF station, and we're made very welcome and join all the other pilots at various receptions, meals, and parties. I learn a great deal about flying lore as we talk during breakfast. We talk while watching the displays; we talk at lunch; and we talk in the evening, when I take these magnificent men out to local restaurants in the town I know well.

It was my first experience of the static line and of meeting the public. I tried to explain my approach to flying, my passion for connections, and my experience flying in the north of Scotland. I had some very interesting conversations. Because my aeroplane was a foreign aircraft, not many people were familiar with its history. There were a few pilots of the RAF, however, who told me how the French adapted the Willy Messerschmitt design for their post-war needs. I listened with bated breath to descriptions of flying vintage aeroplanes, De Havilland Rapides and Puss Moths, and I wished I'd heard the stories before I tried to fly my old aeroplane.

We returned to Prestwick on Sunday. I was flying the aeroplane home to Prestwick from the left-hand seat. Taxiing through million-pound fighters was very new for me, especially with a Scottish haar over everything. I could see Declan counting up the damage if we clouted anything. Luckily, we had a good take off and climbed out of the haar without any problems. Inland, it was blue sky, not unlike the day of the memorial flight. I felt so happy to be an artist and pilot. I was also happy that I had not become a fighter pilot, which had been an ambition of mine long ago. Scotland gleamed with patches of haar and sun, which gave the landscape a prehistoric look as we sped home on our pterodactyl.

Rudolph Hess Film – Edinburgh Festival

I'm sitting in a cinema next to a famous film director. It's the Edinburgh Film Festival in 2006 at Cineworld, and it's the premiere of *Ruchenlage,* the story of Rudolf Hess. We watch the four short documentaries about lies, and I'm absolutely entranced. The famous director James D Pennybaker watches *Ruchenlage,* leans over, and says, "That is an austere film, excellent, excellent." He's right. Astrid and company have spent hours and hours editing this short film. I am filled with admiration for their discipline and selection. My paintings seem extravagant and self-indulgent, my images and imagination so voluptuous and idiosyncratic compared to the almost grey images of the night and the loneliness of the North Sea.

I remember how cold it was over the Irish Sea on that night in May 2006. Ian, the cameraman, wanted the canopy pulled back so that his camera would be unobstructed. The draught freezes round us as we sit tight and still.

The Scottish coast and Ayrshire look quite sinister, as they would have looked to Rudolf Hess. Tone, texture, colour, and composition may be the language of painting, but film uses them to produce such theatrical power. We sense the nature of Hess's lies when we remember his claim that he made this flight in the name of peace mothers and dead children. Meanwhile, Hess was busy helping Hitler with the final solution.

The simple movement of a propeller in the film also dramatises the aeroplane in an understated way. I am filled with admiration for Astrid's use of the parachute. I know they were thinking of photographing a skydiver, but somehow the parachute on the ground – bending over some marsh grass – is all that's needed to indicate the drama. Ian lies in the back of the aeroplane, and the swinging door and cockpit structure is terrifyingly unstable and upside down. The aeroplane never leaves the ground! I think cinema has the capacity to awe its viewers. One's imagination and dreams are caught in time in the dark. Drama needs this confrontation, and it's wonderful to experience a story told so economically.

Our filming from the air creates the background for the archive film on Hess. We hear he wanted to be the new Führer for the Fourth Reich. As Winston Churchill says at the very last second of the film, "Hess or no Hess, I'm watching the Marx Brothers."

Every Minute of the Shortest Flight

Ruchenlage inspired me to find the film I really wanted to make:

Every Minute of the Shortest Flight.

It's a life flying aeroplanes.
heart groans,
heart beats,
heart surges
to excitements

fear of flying,
snakes and ladders,
ancient sunlight
light the land
textures grow and die
every minute of the shortest flight.

reading Saint-Exupéry
oh, these dreams
touching the flying machine
for the first time
a first kiss in a warm country near
the Mediterranean Sea.

Islay 19 August 2007

A former student of mine, Stephen Barclay, comes over to Islay with me for the Islay community's flying show. There is also a fifty-year commemoration of a tragic accident in the flying doctor service. In 1957, the crew of the air ambulance were killed in bad weather, and relatives are invited and flown in to commemorate a plaque to be unveiled that very afternoon.

We hear dire warnings about the weather two days before, but there is a change just in time, and we have clear, breezy, sparkling light that may allow us to use our vertical camera in a creative way.

We set off early, 10:08 a.m., and we arrive at Islay Airport at 10:41 a.m. I land on runway 31 - and its other end R/W 13 will play a part in our film. I set up the vertical camera, not forgetting to wipe its little face clean, and off goes Declan for his display. He flies just right for the rhythm and tempo of the day and the textures of light and shade.

The camera starts with abstract shapes difficult to discern: simple textures of tarmac and concrete. Faster and faster, we see the runway and the markings. A shape then creeps in the side of the frame. A shadow of the undercarriage and the propeller nose, but only suggesting an aerial body- a presence. The shape fades away as the surface of Islay comes into focus. We see the beach and the amazing peat-coloured stream cutting through the beach and the skin surface of the sea itself. The aeroplane eases into the frame with its urgent silhouette and its machine virility coming into centre frame for a few seconds. The light is everything. The textures grow and die every minute of the shortest flight. Snakes and ladders must be the most brilliant game of chance ever. It's just like life.

Alan's soundtrack catches these mysterious movements wonderfully. The Gaelic voiceover doesn't try to describe anything; he's just the trying to convey the feeling of being alive on an island. Meanwhile, the numbers of the runways seem so manufactured, so secure in the passing charade. The aeroplane is never seen in the whole film; instead, there's a sense that we are groping around, rising and falling, nearer and farther, failing and succeeding, but moving always moving. I'm enraptured.

What a wonderful medium film is. I've watched all the BBC's "Coast" films, but their cameras all seem like strangers and something seems missing. I'm reminded of people asking me, "What or who is *The Naked Pilot*?" I reply, "It's an idea that came from a lot of disparate sources. I really wanted to do an art exhibition called *Naked Pilot.* I wanted to use paintings, prints, sculpture, and a film to bring all the ideas together."

I also considered a book. My mother, at the age of 80, wrote a book detailing her early life. This brought home to me just how vulnerable women and men are. "*The Naked Pilot*, then, was somebody who was vulnerable but takes on life with courage. I started a series of prints, some with text describing something about the lives of Amy Johnson, Bill Burns, and Antoine de Saint-Exupéry. It came together in a variety of ways, mostly paintings and a series of ten prints.

The first *Naked Pilot* I came across was in the very first book I took out of Larkhall Public Library: *Don Quixote* by Cervantes. I liked it because of the pictures a knight in armour with his horse and his squire, but I soon realised (even at my very young age) that there was a play on what he thought was happening and reality – it was ironic, satirical, and a wonderful combination of innocence and courage that he used to deal with all life's problems. I began to realise that the naked pilot was a combination of innocence with a cruel exposure to life's problems. I also realised that we all have *Naked Pilots* within us.

During the Islay display, I'm asked to do a commentary. I tell the story of finding the Nord (or perhaps it found me), finding parts, finding a place to rebuild it, and employing the trial-and-error naked pilot approach. I applaud Declan's flying as he tries to forge a connection between what we're doing and all those thinking and seeing minds on the earth below. I would love to install a CCTV in MD and communicate to the audience as things are happening. Maybe they could communicate with the plane, too.

I try to indicate that I'm just an ordinary flying club pilot, not some superman aviator. The atmosphere on Islay that Saturday afternoon is magic, and calendar or watch time didn't mean anything. A few minutes are interminable, and the moments grow in my psyche and imagination in wonderful ways.

Oban! Robert and I leave the smoking and dripping aeroplane and have a cup of tea. It's a strange feeling after three seasons of flying the Nord to be adrift with the mindset of flying back home fractured. "When's the next bus to Glasgow?" I ask.

The fire brigade members are very excited. I think this is the first emergency since the new development of Oban Airport and all its new equipment. I remember it way back in the seventies, when Mr McIntyre's cottage was the *C* in *Control.*

The aeroplane has a nappie wrapped underneath the oily engine and it is parked in an area where the surface is specially designed for spillage.

I didn't bring any covers, but everybody is helpful: we improvise a cockpit cover. I hope the cylinder head can be replaced and the aeroplane flown home in a day or two. My bus pass comes in handy and Robert and I catch the bus with our minds still in the sky. Its thirty-five minutes by air but five and a half hours by bus to Prestwick.

I stop working on my strange LE Velocette and get out my spare aeroplane engines. I have three Renault 6Q engines in various sheds at home in Skelmorlie. Two were recovered from a farm, and one was recovered from an aeroplane in the field. Two with engines had their log books.

Years ago, I carefully dismantled the engine from the aeroplane found in the field. To do this, I built a bench out of art school timber (used for degree shows) and two swivel brackets that allowed me to turn the engine round on its long axis. Inverted engines need this type of set-up because the cylinders go one way and the sump goes another way.

I bought an enormous five-gallon drum of inhibiting oil and eventually put the engine away, wrapped in its oily dream. My engineer is Adnan Sojieri of Prestwick Engineers. I've known Adnan since about 1993. He took up my project of rebuilding the Nord when all the other aircraft engineers in Scotland thought it was an impossible mission. He has a good sense of humour and a high tolerance for mad ideas.

We decided to get back to Oban. I had detached all the parts from my spare number five cylinder head, four crankcase studs, gaskets and a rusty sparkplug or two.

I travelled back up to Oban with my flight bag and hoped I'd be flying the aircraft home the next evening.

Adnan and Stuart were there at 9:00 a.m., and we uncovered MD and opened the engine covers. The engineers were appalled at the sight of the sparkplug dangling over the carburettors, but on the other side of the engine, Adnan found a crack in the crankcase, which meant there would be no quick repair that day. In fact, the engine was essentially useless. And so we went back to the drawing board. (We learned later that the broken end of the connecting rod had jammed between the rod and the crankcase, and the vicious pressure had cracked the side of the engine.)

I thought *where can I put this wounded bird so we can take the engine down to Prestwick and repair it with all my spares?* The gliding club hangar was the most promising, location, and we had to take off the wing tips and the radio aerials to squeeze it in. The gliders had enormous wings, but they sat on trolleys before being pushed in sideways with their 40-ft wings located up and down the hangar. The Nord looked very happy in her new nest.

LE VELO

The LE Velo always had a Birmingham accent. I phone LE Club, and the voice at the other end always has the same accent. Whatever's wrong with my bike is the same thing that has hindered their bikes for years.

The LE seems to be able to run well for about five minutes before it begins to misfire and lose power. It runs slower and slower, and finally – even when the clutch is pulled in – the revs don't rise as they should. I try to use this five or ten-minute running time to get myself to the pub just down the road. It's a beautiful, cold day, and Sunday lunch is about enough time for my strange bike to cool and gather its strength for the return journey.

The pub fraternity heads out to watch me make it home. But a Velocette never lets you down, and with one pull of the handstart, the bike burbles to life. I have the same ten-minute running time, but it's difficult to get up the hill to Skelmorlie. The next day, I get close to the same results, but I'm able to travel a bit farther and a bit faster. I actually overtook a cyclist!

There's something about the engine that seems to be improving. I ponder, *Could it be something dreadfully subtle such as the fact that the flywheel has lost its magnetism? I did take it off to repair the oil seal; perhaps it was outside of the motorcycle for too long.* Gordon in Worsley told me he had the same problem. He stopped the bike, had a fag, and after twenty minutes, his Valiant was ready for anything. *Perhaps it's the coil,* I muse. Gordon tells me he's going to send his spare coil up to Scotland. I also replace the condenser and the points and the exhaust pipes. I'm trying anything I can think of.

After my fourth run in four days, I decide I've earned some shopping. This time I feel some power in the bike – though, from time to time, the running becomes very rich and heavy. I find that the choke hasn't had a little bend put in, and it's vibrating to fully rich. I lean down and push it back to normal. This time, there's a motorcycle on the road, but I zoom up the hill with no problems. Wow! The bike almost seems back to normal at last.

Snow arrives, and freezing fog is not motorcycle weather, but I consider running the LE for an hour or so. The snow settles on the high ground over the sea. I wrap up in jumpers and scarves and my Mk V111 goggles, and off I go to climb Knockhill. The LE handles beautifully, and the plan is to go fast downhill, round the bend at the bottom of the hill, and zoom up the climb. There are only three gears – the middle gear is useful, but the first gear is usually needed before the brow of the hill, where it all starts again down the next hill. The LE looks terrific left parked in the snow on a rough track. I leave my motorcycle clothes in the panniers and head up the mountain.

It's not a very big mountain, but the snow is slippery and as I try to find a good place for coffee flask and tortillas, I test gravity slightly and end up in a glissade that the motorcycle would be proud of. As it darkens, I clomp down the hill, over the moor, and there is my temperamental LE. *Will she start?* I think I've got carburettor icing more often seen in aeroplanes with the same flat, horizontally-oriented engine and exposed carburettors. I let the bike run down the steep track and let the clutch in. It takes a yard or two, but up she fires, stops, and fires again. The warmer air provides a healthy mixture, and we're headed home. How satisfying! It's that obstacle that Saint-Exupéry talks about: "The earth teaches us more about ourselves than all the books because it resists us. Man discovers himself when he measures himself against the obstacle." I await my new spare parts for the next drama with the obstacle.

Idea of Rebuilding the Nord 1101

propellers still
propellers fast
lights on
lights off
torsos gleaming in the sun
little heads and staring eyes,
staring eyes

Fuselage Dismantled by Jim Hardie, 1995

Riveting is riveting. I carefully cut the rivet to the exact size and put it in the drilled hole. The dolly goes behind it, and the compressed air gun is gently brought up against the head of the rivet. My left wrist contorts painfully with the heavy dolly and tenses the left side of my stretched-out torso while my right hand gently and sensitively presses the gun on target. As I activate the machine, the very first touch of the gun is enough to make the rivet disappear instantly. I hear the faintest *ping* as gravity takes it to the graveyard that is the floor of the shed. I swear and start again. *Only another thousand or two to go,* I think.

The stub wings have a plywood layer underneath the aluminium skin. How do you cut these wooden shapes so that the tiny rivets go through the three skins (metal, wood, metal)? The rivets tend to bend if the dolly is not perfectly square to the rivet. It's fascinating to make cardboard patterns and build sections up.

A flying machine! The aeroplane's log book tells the story of this aeroplane: amazing trips over to France (for example, Thruxton–Montelimar, Montelimar–Cannes, Cannes–Thruxton, Thruxton–Dinard, Dinard–Thruxton, Thruxton–Cherbourg, Thruxton–Guernsey.

A Mr Collins seems to be the pilot. His widow eventually contacts me and tells me his amazing story. She wants to see DB again and travels up to Prestwick where it's still very much in pieces but with a new main spar. During the Second World War, Mr Collins was an agent in France and had come to know France very well. His journeys in DB must have been something else in the seventies. In the remarks column are curt notes on strong headwinds and weather problems, IFR, and the odd shimmy problem. The aeroplane seems to have run very well for him with a total of almost a hundred and fifty hours of flight time in less than three years. Unfortunately, I never met him and can only attempt to conjure up the connections he was making in the last years of his adventurous life.

I get my first muscular spasm. Being tensed over a job such as riveting is not good for one. My back muscles go into spasm, and my joints start to ache. I start to have cramps at night and can't get to sleep. *Am I identifying too much with old motorcycles and older aeroplanes? How did I get into this?* The Glasgow School of Art helped. We made A-frames to suspend the fuselage and work underneath it. I had an old ratchet winch and a few nylon slings, but my position was a bit precarious. Joe Walker, a retired aircraft engineer from Perth, gave me a lot of his time. He and his wife came down from Perth to Skelmorelie, and we worked out how to replace the corroded main spar. Eddie Edwards, another engineer, brought along his tools and loaned me his spare riveting gun and dollies.

There was one spectacular crash when the steel wire rope unwound from my boy-scout knots and let the whole fuselage crash to the floor of our garage/hangar. From then on, we always had proper trestles and kept the fuselage at one angle.

I sprayed the clean metal with a wonderful, painterly khaki-green rust inhibiter undercoat, and the great day arrived when we took one wall of the shed down and rolled DB out into the lawn at Skelmorelie. It faced the sea spectacularly, and it pointed at

Rothesay and the Kyle's of Bute. It didn't have wings, but without an engine or propeller it had the look of a sculpture pointing into the eye of the wind towards the sea. But it was still on the ground.

So many people want to help. I hear of many similarly daft projects. When the CAA members come to inspect the parts and check off the numbers and certificates; they ask me to lay them out on the lawn. It all looks very amateur. But the inspectors say they've seen much stranger examples.

There was the farmer in Yorkshire who somehow or another had a Vickers Viscount airliner in his field. He met the inspectors with great bonhomie, "Lads, we're nearly there! My tractor man is good wi' bits an' pieces. Come back next week an' it'll be ready to go!"

My oldest pal, Bobbie McGregor from Larkhall, runs a blacksmith business in Larkhall called Marchbanks, and he has been a devotee of flying all his life. Bobby and I met in 1943 in Union Street Primary School (now Glengowan). I remember distinctly sitting beside him at a desk, and we were both drawing aeroplanes. We wanted to be Spitfire pilots. I kept on drawing aeroplanes, but Bobby did something a bit more useful: he got a degree in metallurgy and became the managing director of Marchbanks near Larkhall Cross. As we passed that blacksmith shop as schoolboys, we smelt for the first time the acrid burning of welding and the smoke and sparks of metalworking. The workmen seemed entirely intent on their work and had no time for small boys. It all looked impressive and dangerous.

Bobby, now a widower, drove down from Larkhall to Skelmorelie and was really useful on the other end, the dolly end, of riveting. It really is a two-man operation. We talked of flying this old classic aeroplane, and it seemed like such a natural progression from the days of Miss Dawson in Union Street Primary School and later Larkhall Academy, which was just across Academy Street at the time. Bobby went into gliding with the Scottish Gliding Club and Strathhaven Gliding Club, and he owned a share in a high-performance glider.

At the time he was doing this, I was flying all over the north-east of Scotland for Aberdeen College of Education. I was visiting graduates on their area investigation weeks of teaching practice. I was a flying tutor who sat through their art lessons and made reports. I also sat in on their critiques on art teaching back at the college in Aberdeen.

In rebuilding the Nord, my big problem was that I lacked a propeller. I had the propeller for DB and a propeller from the farm, but both were very corroded. It must perform a very sophisticated job, the Ratier propeller. The propeller can be moved from coarse to fine manually. Switched to automatic, the propeller sets itself. The manifold pressure is very important, and when in cruise/arret, we should have 80 hpa, 2,300 rpm, and 120 knots (about 140 mph). It's a very fragile electrical system that works well, and in dreich, wet, old Scotland, I often wonder about these old electrical brushes and connections.

The famous ME 109 fighter has the same propeller system I saw sitting in the cockpit of René Meyer's 109 in Livry Gargan (still in the basement, thank God). This allows acceleration from changes of pitch like changing down in a manual gearbox – that's supposed to be an advantage in combat, but I'll just take René's word for that!

Where can I get a Ratier propeller? I wonder. Pam and I search about and discover just one spare. It's down in North Weald, but unfortunately, it is attached to an aeroplane. And seemingly nobody sells a propeller without the rest of the aeroplane if that's even a remote possibility. This particular aeroplane is an earlier model than mine, but it has the same engine, a Renault 6Q. It's a Nord 1001, a traildragger. Seemingly, there's quite a few Nords about, but they all have one thing in common: no port wing. The old engineer tells me that the Messerschmitts had problems landing, and both the 109 and the 108 tended to ground loop. Even back in the thirties, when aerodromes had the wind sock in the middle of the field and one could land straight into wind. Now, of course, with fixed runways, nearly all landings are a bit crosswind, so a traildragger with a narrow track, retractable undercarriage, and a great, heavy engine seems likely to self-destruct if it lands and turns sharply in on itself … always to port, in this case. I think, *if I have to buy a propeller attached to a fuselage, perhaps I should look for a fuselage that's the same as my Nord 1101.* Eventually, I manage to buy the propeller with the rest of the aeroplane tacked on. This is G-BSMD

The body seems to make its own connections – tensions as the work goes up and down. Only millionaires rebuild vintage aeroplanes; keeping up a pilot's licence via a trial-and-error, naked pilot approach is tricky.

All this time spent in a strange world. I paint away at all the stages of the dismantling, repainting, rebuilding, determining, and keeping up the pilot's license. We start Real Artists Partnerships and travel to the Far East for projects. I'm fascinated by Wilbur Wright and my naked pilots: Amy Johnson, Bill Burns, and Saint-Exupéry.

Spare Parts List by Jim Hardie, 2007

But things go wrong. The stress is too much for Pam, and she leaves. Poor, old, corroded DB is not a good bet to found a flying Aerolab on, so when I see a propeller-attached aeroplane that is kept in a heated hangar, I begin to wonder.

Like all my rebuilds of classic motorcycles and cars, it's going to be the Christmas tree technique again. This is where the best of the parts available are bolted on like presents on a Christmas tree. It seems extravagant to buy this aeroplane, but it means there is a great bank of spares from almost three Nords … and I have the feeling we're going to need them.

I go to doctors, chiropractors, and osteopaths for my aches and pains. But the general view in the west of Scotland is as follows: "What do you expect at your age when rebuilding an aeroplane. Why don't you just sit in the pub and drink happily like the rest of us."

I suppose the stress builds up more living on your own, and eventually, I seem stuck in bed with more cramps in my joints and a very bad back. It seems the flying and the rebuilding must come to an end. I can't even walk the dog. What's to be done?

Enter *Dr Campbell's Home Cure for Osteoarthritis.* This is a very small book I find in Skelmorlie Library, a library much the size of my living room. Dr Campbell tells me he can cure me in three days. The problem, he says, is nutrition. He insists on a seven-day menu and they I must stick to for at least three months. Here are the first three days. For day one, fast and drink at least four glasses of water (bottled or spring water if possible). For day two, unsweetened grape or prune juice and bananas for breakfast; fresh beef liver (preferably raw or lightly sautéed), a mixed greens salad with oil and cider vinegar dressing, and a bowl of blackberries or other seasonal fruit for lunch; a raw vegetable plate (green peppers, celery, for example), a raw fruit salad (shredded apples, figs, grapes, bananas, etc. – but no citrus fruits) for dinner along with one tablespoon of cod liver oil twice per day. For day three, blended raw fruits and a glass of milk for breakfast; fresh fillet of lightly sautéed ocean fish, raw cauliflower or other raw vegetables, a glass of milk with one tablespoon of powdered brewer's yeast, and a tablespoon of blackstrap molasses for lunch; fresh beef liver lightly sautéed with onions, a mixed greens salad, melon or other seasonal fruit, and a glass of milk for dinner (along with one tablespoon of cod liver oil twice per day).

The complete fast is a new experience for me. I drink plenty of water, but strangely enough, I don't feel all that hungry. It brings home just how much we put into our stomachs every twenty-four hours. In some ways, we become anaesthetised to these repeated feelings of hunger and thirst. I love bread and eat about one loaf per day with marvellous fillings for my sandwiches, but bread can be full of chemicals. I have to break these habits and think again.

On the second day, there is no change. I follow the plan to the letter, but my cramps, sore back, and general stiffness are still there. I can barely get out of bed to go to the bathroom. On the third day, I'm confined to bed feeling sorry for myself. The poor dog, Stormy, a beautiful Gordon Setter, stays with me and empathises. He does get out now and again. The afternoon passes, and when the night comes down, I wonder why I took this last chance so seriously.

At about two o'clock in the morning, I wake up and feel different. A funny sort of glow seems to start in my middle and spread down to my knees and up to my chest. A feeling of lightness and looseness comes over me, and I feel alert, too. I move gingerly, bringing my knees up and trying to turn onto my side. I wait for the pain, but it doesn't come. I put my legs over the bed and try to let my knees slide down to the floor. My knees touch the floor, but I still feel good. *What am I creeping around like this for?* I wonder. I stand up slowly, then, and walk. I walk more. I move about and dance. I'm completely cured and feel 100 per cent. It's the first cure I've ever seen work in my whole life.

When I go for the medical examination for my pilot's licence, my eyesight, my blood pressure, my general fitness, and my reflexes, are deemed excellent by the CAA doctor.

Tail Plane Nord 1101, 1995

My concentration improves, and over the next two or three months, I lose twenty-eight pounds. *How will my concentration stand up to flying?* I wonder. Over the last several years, my flying has become less frequent. Flying clubs have been trying to build up a habit of practising for a certain amount of hours every month. But rebuilding aeroplanes is the classic distraction from flying them. I've heard all sorts of stories of homebuilt aircraft that seem very unfamiliar in the air. The difference between aeroplanes on the ground and in the air is enormous.

After building my cardboard simulator and taking in plenty of information, I really want a flight or two with a pilot familiar with the aeroplane. I suppose the usual thing is the former owner who can pass on his experience to the new owner. In my case, none of the aeroplanes can fly and haven't flown for years, so it's back to the cardboard simulator.

Unfortunately, the ferry flight from North Weald to Prestwick is a one-off. Finding an experienced pilot is difficult in Scotland. Confidence is the great thing when landing an aeroplane alongside a certain amount of conversion training. Try as I might, though, I just can't find the conversion training. Is it in the cards to fly it back to Scotland with all the information but very little experience actually flying it? A foreign aeroplane is different. I did have a chance to fly a Nord in France, but restrictions were put on these classics by the French government, and my friend, René Meyer, tried hard to give me some experience, but it just didn't work out. I had flown the aircraft before, but from the right-hand seat and not with a flying instructor. And so the famous *sink* didn't quite get through to me when I landed the aircraft smoothly with Martin on the throttle. I did make the point that I would have liked about twenty hours of conversion, but I didn't know where to get it.

The great unknown, I find, is the pilot's equilibrium at the particular time of flying. Distractions come in every form. The CAA are bringing out all sorts of DVDs on typical accidents that can arise from many sources: arguments with the wife, press-on macho behaviour, flying with a cold, trying to do too much in a hurry on your own. I think, too, of the phrase on many flying club walls: "Are you flying the aeroplane you think you are?" I found the Nord so different from the aeroplanes I had flown for over thirty years. I felt my confidence go down when comparing my skills to the commercial pilots I eventually flew.

Patience is needed, but I wouldn't recommend the cardboard cut-out school of flying! Once a few successful landings and flights are made, the whole venture seems wonderful. The character of the thirties and forties as expressed by the classic aeroplane is well worth the mysterious conversion, especially if it's a foreign one. I wouldn't fly anything else now.

The next connection is a portrait of the Sojeeri family. It's like singing for your supper. I'll paint their portrait for my usual fee, but this fee will be bartered for the price of rebuilding the new engine. Adnan has his B licence, and with his young apprentices, he will do a fantastic job on the Renault 6Q. I want to have a hands-on working with the engine, so I plan to make the gaskets (a skill I learned rebuilding classic motorcycles).

In the painting, I want to develop the engineers' role in flying. I'm going to use the Nord as the foreground, middle distance, and background to the six human beings in the portrait. I design the painting carefully around the aeroplane, trying to bring out the relationships between the husband, wife, two younger children, and two older children. Everybody works at the flying club; everybody lives and breathes aeroplanes. As they should!

Watching the engineers cleaning off any small particles of corrosion from the replacement engine, I am reminded of my naked pilots, Bill Burns and Saint-Exupéry. Burns worked away in his studio at Newmacher with a kind of desperate concentration on his images. Influenced by Bill Scott, he was consumed with creating flat patterns that distilled huge emotions. What Bill Scott did with pots and pans, Bill Burns did with harbours, boats, mines, breakwaters, and sea walls. I remember him telling me about his working method: he would mix up his quantities of oil paint for the areas of pattern and image in his painting, and if the quantity ran out before the shape was painted, he would scrape off the paint and go back to the beginning and start mixing the colour again. He was concentrated so hard that he would paint right through the night. He felt he had to get it right no matter what it took. His ulcer could leave him in a terrible state, though, and before he crashed his aeroplane, he told everybody he felt he didn't want to last beyond fifty years. But his quote, "I've put something there that wasn't there before" says it all.

Saint-Exupéry had this same dedication to his craft, but a very different working method. He sat in cafes and wrote and rewrote. He couldn't sleep and was known to pick up a phone directory and randomly phone people to read his latest chapter aloud to them. This occurred, at times, at around two o'clock or three o'clock in the morning. As I work on these memoirs, I feel I must find out more about writing.

Night Flight by James Hardie, 1993

I'm looking at my classic LE Velocette. There's something about it. I go over the plugs, the choke on the carburettor. I adjust the brakes and the throttle. I feel confident I'll be able to ride it to Largs, and if all goes well, I'll go for a real run.

The snow and sleet stops and allows the sun to come out. There's a lot of water on the roads, and the flood signs are out. The bike starts revving quickly because the throttle is set too wide. No more retard, so I let the clutch in and the engine pulls really well. The bike continues to run well as I continue along the coast road (the inland roads are still icy). We tour along at about 40 mph. Every van, lorry, and car passes us – to pass a motorcycle seems to be an ambition of everything on four wheels. I pass through Fairlie and move towards West Kilbride. I see the sign for Portencross and turn down towards the clachan of Portencross. This is, of course, where my fellow artist and old friend Alasdair Taylor lived and brought up his children. I see Geoff's cottage and engineering shop. He was a friend of Alasdair's and lives a life that combines his love for boats, exotic cars, and motorbikes. He maintains them through his own business. They gave me a wonderful cup of mushroom soup and tell me their tale of woe. Geoff's just been banned from driving for two years, and this has happened right when he has his most exotic collection of huge, powerful cars. The cars look quite surreal against the textures of rocks, sea cliffs, and the glittering salt air.

How connections with machinery can break down. I think of my trouble with the Nord and the ghastly feeling of bereavement I've felt when I had to leave a machine behind in some unfamiliar environment. What is Geoff going to do with his AC cobras, his Harley Davidson, and his Ford Mustang? I wonder.

The cold comes down quite early in the afternoon as the sun disappears, and I get started on my LE. Even at 40 mph, I feel very cold. I remember, over twenty years ago, finding this particular LE in a smaller clachan of Pinminnoch near Girvan. It had belonged to a well-known artist, Sinclair Thomson, who had died and left his favourite bike in a barn near his cottage.

It was a favourite of Sinclair's because Sinclair only had one leg. He had a bad break when playing rugby at the age of 18, and that break never really healed. He was still in pain long after the amputation. Sinclair had connected with this LE Velo because the LE had a hand start and a hand change. In fact, there was only one foot brake, on the left-hand side.

When I first found the bike, I couldn't get it fired up at all. I examined it carefully and saw that, next to the handlebars, there was a box lid for the toolbox. Inside the box were three half crowns, which in the eighties, seemed very unfamiliar. Opening the two pear-shaped panniers at the rear wheel, I found a nest of papers and rags in the shape of whisky bottle. Of course, three half crowns would be the price of a whisky bottle back in 1953, and that was Sinclair's answer to the nagging pain coming from his leg. Now I begin to wonder about the stories of Sinclair riding the LE down the long steps of Garnethill. Garnethill was the Montmartre of Glasgow, and it still has the steep steps today. Good for you, Sinclair Thomson. The LE goes well and back to Skelmorlie. What else could it do?

First Aerial Voyage in Scotland

Vincenzo Lunardi Drawing James Hardie, 2007

I'm told a wonderful story in St Andrews in the arts group office. It's the story of the first aerial voyage in Scotland, of a man taking to the air as a flying "mortal" - not an airy object - a poltergeist, a spirit - but like you and me flesh and blood - an actual human being.

The year was 1785. Rabbie Burns was an up-and-coming poet with about eleven years to live. France was threatening on the continent, and religion had the human spirit tied to God-fearing sin in the face of every dream or creative thought. How did a young Italian dare?

He did dare, though, and I was sent forth from the arts office on a sunny Saturday to seek his memory. I drove to Cupar and took the Peat Inn road to Pitscottie. I'm told to go through Pitscottie and drive up a steep hill. At a sharp bend, I'm instructed to park the car and get out and look behind the hedge. And there it is: "Here on the 8th of October 1785, Vincent Lunardi alighted after the first flight in Scotland." That was 223 years ago. What a connection.

He even flew over Larkhall the next month on 23 November 1785. His route was St Andrews Square, Glasgow, Hamilton, Lanark, and down to the borders at Hawick. To set an example for aviation on the third flight in December, he crashed near the Isle of May in the Firth of Forth. After a while in the sea, he was rescued by a passing fisherman. This set the seal on things to come.

The other strange phenomenon was the reaction by the populace in the eighteenth century. Passion was unleashed in scenes of hysterical enthusiasm for flying. If the aeronauts didn't produce the goods, the crowd took over and did their best to wreck the place. Pop culture had its birth there in Edinburgh and Glasgow. Even Lindberg and Amy Johnson were foreseen. It was the first mobbing of heroes of our time!

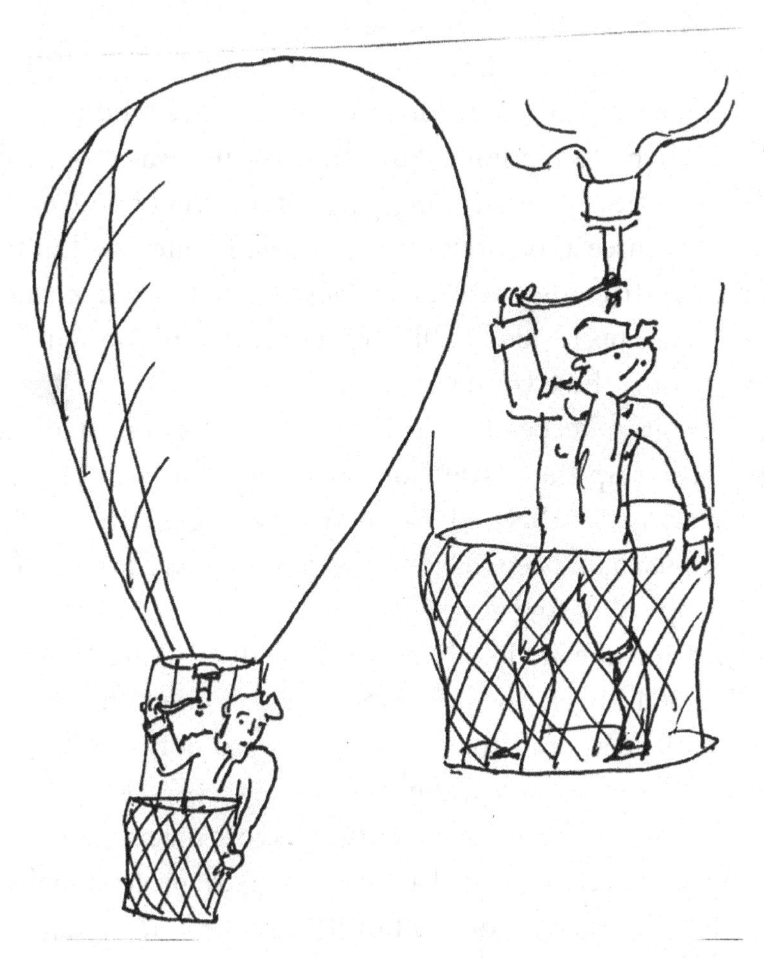

Vincenzo Lunardi Drawing by James Hardie, 2007

Standing on that hill at Pitlessie, I draw some images for my theatre of the skies. Could I use the Nord as a theatre, a dramatic working of this story? I try a line or two: "My name is Vincenzo Lunardi. I am a young man. Already, I am secretary to the Prince of Caramanico of the Neapolitan Court. I am going to be famous. Now, in 1785,

I am going to be the first to fly in Scotland. How everybody adores me, especially the young Scottish ladies in Glasgow and Edinburgh. They adore me and say I make their gentlemen admirers as dull as dust clinging to the planet!"

The connection though, really interests me – the connection to 2008. Where are these 1785 ravers? I talk about the idea in the village where I live, Skelmorlie. The Skelmorlie Villagers know all about aeronauts and their devilish contrivances. This is the village where I tried to rebuild my Nord. I swore at vanishing rivets and wheeled my flying machine out to tackle the world of art. I met a librarian, Grace, who constantly searched for books. Caroline, the postmistress, eyed my strange packets with a glint in her eye. Hugh, the greenkeeper, filmed *Aeroplane for a Naked Pilot.* He set the scene for future adventure. Hugh was brilliant at taking down the walls of the shed and putting them back as we moved the aeroplane yet again.

The flying club at Prestwick wanted to tell the world just what they had to put up with. I asked for references and connections to the idea of rebuilding a classic aeroplane and I certainly got them. Receptionist Suzanne's picture was more about Stormy the flying dog than about me. Adnan, the engineer, on the other hand, offered some really intelligent ideas: "My three apprentices are particularly interested in the plane and its early monocoque construction, retractable tricycle undercarriage, and unusual pitch propeller. The engine is upside down, like the aeroplanes of the thirties. It is a unique opportunity for training these young men."

I took Hugh, the greenkeeper, flying. The weather was poor that summer day, and we couldn't get too far up the Clyde, but low clouds and rain really brought home the era of the thirties and the Second World War to Hugh. He said, "I really began to realise just what it must have been like for these young men having to fly in such crude machinery with people shooting at them."

Ian Shearman from the Rudolf Hess research days wrote from a very different point of view: "In 2004 Mr Hardie asked me to contribute to his Aerolab project. He had renovated a vintage aircraft that he aimed would not only become an arts and cultural resource, but also act as a stimulus for other artists. My role was to carry out photofinishing and montage of materials for the project's official launch, an opportunity that confirmed my previously untested ability to work to professional standards. I was also involved in the general development of the project and its launch, and thus can attest to Mr Hardies' inclusive approach. I suffer from mental illness and have seldom enjoyed opportunities to express my abilities.

"In conclusion, I feel it is important to assert that, although I do not share Mr Hardies' enthusiasm for flying as such, I certainly believe in the human fascination with flight. When flying, we have a different perception, something at the root of artistic creation. Therefore it seems evident that any project concerned with flying has the potential to galvanize not only individuals, but groups and communities. Until I met Mr Hardie, I did not realise that Scotland was so intrinsic to the history of flight."

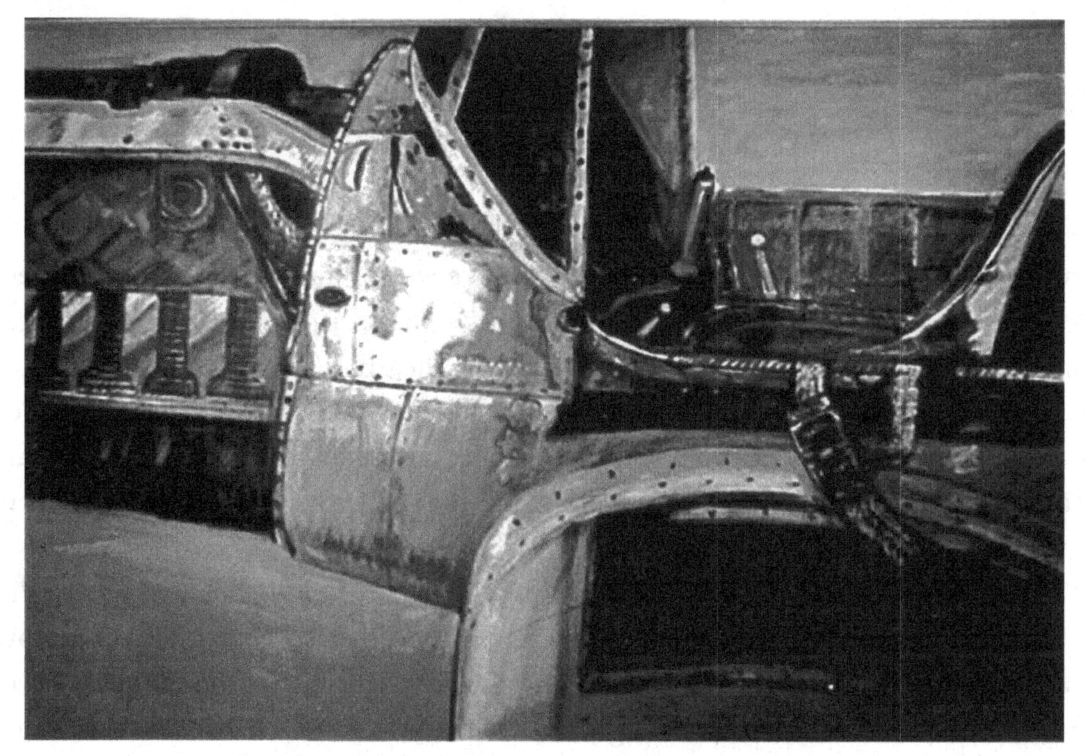

Fuselage Nord 1101 by James Hardie, 1995

Wright Brothers - Motorcycling

How are we connected to the aeroplane? How are we connected to anything? There's one phrase: "*C'est un peu, dans chacun de ces hommes, Motzart assasine.*" It's from Saint-Exupéry's *Terre des Hommes.* What does it mean? We don't know how we are connected to anything, but the opposite is dangerous. If we deliberately don't connect, it's like something dies. Saint-Exupéry found an icon in a small Polish boy who became a potential Motzart. Somehow, this child stood for the enormous carelessness of the unconnected.

There were terrible disconnections among the itinerant Polish workers travelling to Russia, travelling back to Poland, worn to the bone by this struggle, beaten down by a mechanised civilisation where the manhood of the pilot, the integrity of the poet and painter found it increasingly difficult to assert itself. The countryman is uprooted and tossed like one more human faggot on to the mounting woodpile of mindless and soulless proletariat, where most poignantly of all, the bright, creative flames such as *The Little Prince* – the Mozart slumbering in each growing child – is snuffed out in the raucous honky-tonk of cheap cafe music and spiritless distractions of an overcrowded, overagitated, infrahuman world where "there is no gardener for men. only the spirit, if it breathe upon clay, can create man (to use the closing words of *Terre des Hommes*).

Seeking Gravity Detail by James Hardie, 2009

In 1939, just before the Second World War was a bright point in Saint-Exupéry's life, he felt the "ownership of his imagination" and described the dehumanisation of these itinerant workers in the terms of the thirties. The Second World War and *Le Debacle* of France were only months away.

In his words: "And so you feel yourself carried away by this internal migration no one ever spoke to you about. Suddenly, by virtue of a midnight test which stripped you of all accessories, you discovered in yourself a person of whom you were unaware. Someone great and whom you will never forget. And it's yourself! He has opened his wings. He is no longer bound to the perishable goods of this world. He has agreed to die for all men and thus entered into something universal. A mighty breath sweeps through him and here he is shed of his matrix, the sovereign lord that lay dormant within you MAN. You are the equal of the musician who composes, of the physicist who broadens the horizon of knowledge. You have reached that altitude where all loves have a common measure. You may have suffered, you may have felt lonely, your body may have found no refuge, but into its open arms today you have been received by love."

In 1944, Saint-Exupéry had disappeared. And at the end of the war many of his terms had disappeared, too, but the disconnections became complex. Many worlds of disconnections became established. Art, though, didn't change the need to connect; it is still paramount. There are so many wonderful ways to try.

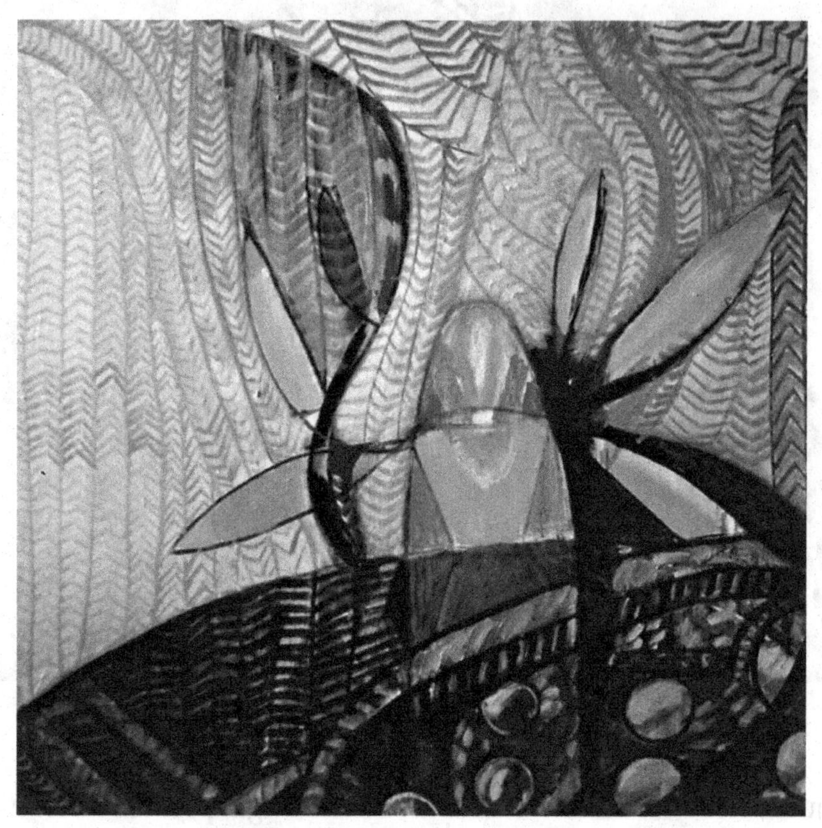

Seeking Gravity (Detail) by James Hardie, 2009

In the Shed Again

All this talk of dynamic forces has brought up the weather. Gales and heavy rain bring life in the sheds to a halt. The west of Scotland has this characteristic of losing itself in the weather – the pervading, salty dampness gets into everything. I remember flying over St Kilda photographing the buildings for an architecture student's dissertation. The most unusual buildings I saw were what I thought were haystacks. They were cone-shaped structures, but they were built of stone with spaces in between each stone. This was the only way of preserving ropes from rotting. The wind whistling through dried out the ropes and gave them a longer life so they could be used to find birds and eggs on the cliffs of Hirta.

The holes in the shed where the aeroplane tail sticks out have the same properties. I open up some more holes, and the Velo, paintings, and aeroplane parts have a drier environment, but only comparatively speaking. As I work on the Velo, I'm amazed that, every day, condensation pours off the metal and makes the rust treatment difficult. I remember reading that, in the fifties; it was all about doing up the bike. The cult of restoration didn't happen until the seventies, when frames were sent away to be powder-coated and everything was restored to new.

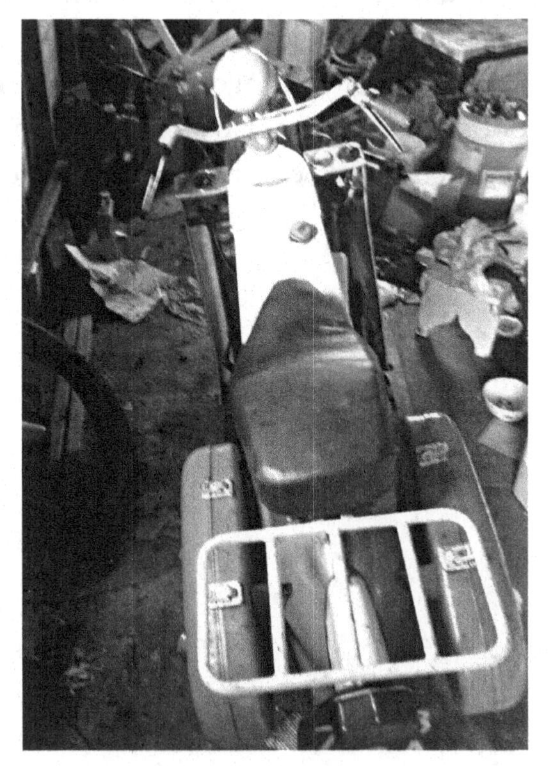

Rebuilding Velocette LE, 2009

Doing up is more my thing, and somehow, the wear and tear characteristics of the old machines are preserved (for a time, at least).

Back in 1959, we lived in a shed – "the hut." After the Second World War, there were converted railway carriages and huts dotted about the landscape. Ex-servicemen spent their famous gratuities on them for some peace and quiet after their service in the forces. They rehabilitated themselves, and their modest country residences were useful to all sorts of misfits well into the fifties and sixties. In fact, small communities grew up here and there and are still going strong.

My first shed belonged to a writer/reporter of the *Glasgow Herald.* Built near the Campsie Hills, it had two rooms and a kitchen with stoves in the rooms and a brick fireplace. There was no water, no gas, no electricity. *La vie de Bohème* at last! The water had to be carried from a farm some 400 yards away, but in the spirit of Wilbur and Orville, I devised a water system for rainwater and advertised for the famous Tilley lamps. These were paraffin pressure lamps that lit a mantle and achieved something like a 60-watt performance with extra heat to take care of the condensation. I searched ***Slamannan*** and Avondale and came away with six. I kept my easel outside where the cattle rubbed their bums on it and deposited a kindly patina on its surface. I never really got away from sheds after that, and I now have three sheds perched over the Kyles of Bute. They are exposed to the weather as all sheds should be. I sense their distress as their roofs leak and bits of roof are blown into the rhododendrons. On a sunny day, however, there's something about them that reminds me of old studios and painting outside among the cows and sheep.

I work away in the howling wind to build a stretcher for a painting. I buy the wood and cut out the half-lap joints, which make a stronger corner than traditional, mitred ends and stretch the canvas. The new acrylic gesso primers are wonderful, and three coats later, I have a brilliant surface to paint on. I can barely remember the glue size and undercoats of years ago. I do remember the glue size going mouldy in the dampness of Scottish studios. No wonder painting was invented in a warm country near the Mediterranean Sea – life on the perimeters of Europe is and was damp.

Youth Hostel Warden in 1957

In the summer of 1957, I was a youth hostel warden and fighting the weather at John O'Groats in the north-east of Scotland. I had travelled up from Inverness to bring to a close the Castletown Youth Hostel. The warden had given up and informed the SYHA that he was ill and needed to return to Edinburgh. The roofs leaked and the beds were damp. Castletown was an old RAF camp for the airfield behind the village and had seen better days. I was 19 and thought that anybody over 21 was well past it, and I said goodbye to the departing Edinburgh student warden who handed me a letter and described the third sand dune on the left at Dunnet Bay as its destination. A lady would be found sitting behind the dune and would appreciate the letter.

The roofs leaked and the beds were wet. The bookings, however, went right through June to September, mostly from students and young travellers from the continent. The Netherlands, France, and Germany ... I had never been there because the Second World War had closed off the continent for so many years. Now these young people had heard of Land's End and John O'Groats and wanted to say they had visited such famous extremities. Were they markers in their sense of Europe, or were they just a rite of passage for hitchhikers? I felt I should try to honour their bookings and repair the hut roofs and dry the beds. Enter Mr Mackay from Castletown, a quiet, powerful ex-seaman. One of his hands were like both of mine together. He removed sound sections of asbestos roofing from huts and replaced the leaky ones on our dormitories. Just by helping him, I felt like I was rounding the horn in good company. I think the whole bill would have been about eight pounds.

I brought all the wet mattresses to the kitchen and dining room hut, and I kept the stove going twenty-four hours per day. Everybody slept in the same hut. I learned more that summer than the previous dozen just how tough it is to be on your own and responsible for the running of a hostel with forty-eight bed. The hostel was very popular and nobody wanted to leave.

I painted the continent. Each different country seemed to become a portrait, and I was the portrait painter. My portrait of the Netherlands was Els Hannekamp, a 17-year-old girl from Zutphen. She was very different to the girls from Larkhall and spoke English with a marvellous, throaty, Dutch accent. My hardboards had followed me round the Highlands as a peripatetic warden and caught up with me in Castletown. The largest board I had primed, but I started the portrait on the textured side of the hardboard. The paint sank in, and I realised it was not like a canvas. Consequently, I had to start again. The Netherlands appeared on this side of the board through an intense pair of blue eyes that seemed to see through all my adolescent pretensions. The portrait won an award at the Royal Scottish Academy in 1958 and was held over to the Edinburgh Festival Exhibition that year. It was hung near Picasso's monumental large figures from some collection loaned for the international exhibition. It was certainly some connection to the continent. Painted in a damp hut and in a rough, student frame, it gave me a marker in my life as an artist. I still have the painting here in Skelmorlie fifty years later.

Painters' Landscape

In 1966, I felt I would never make another film. *A Painter's Landscape* had just been born, and as a product of the Royal College of Art in London. My friends, Oscar Marzaroli and Andrew McTaggart, had come out to Fife Ness at the very eastern extremity of Fife to make a film about the act of art.

I had been painting for years at Fife Ness. The tides moving around the rock formations seemed to create a Lilliputian world of its own. I wondered, *Can film in these days – a 16 mm celluloid business made with enormous cameras – bring man and his art back into connection?*

I asked for help. Andrew McTaggart was an English teacher at Kirkcaldy Junior High School. He decided to give it all up and become a filmmaker, and he got a place in The Royal College of Art Film School. He would make the proposed film part of his student work. He brought along Paul Watson, who became famous as a documentary producer with the BBC. In 1974, Watson made "The Family" a renowned production. Also, he brought photographer Oscar Marzaroli fame for his iconic images of Glasgow in the 1960s. We descended on Fife Ness with all sorts of equipment, including a large canoe that served as a camera dolly, by floating serenely around the pools of seawater. I was Hardie by name and hardy by nature in those days, and I stood chest-deep in the sea while guiding and pointing the canoe with the camera and cameraman attached.

As a painter, I was not used to waiting around in the act of art. This was new for me, and my impatience must have been trying for the film crew. Waiting for the weather (again), waiting for the light, collecting people (from Glasgow, London, and Fife), and getting the right camera. Making the right film is much different than painting a canvas.

It was a relief to get it all down to the RCA in London. We hired a car and drove down. I stayed with Paul Watson and his wife out at Clapham Common. It was fascinating to see the RCA film department up close. The student films were very contemporary, mostly grainy, black and white pieces. Andrew McTaggart's film was in colour, and the shots of Pictish Stones and Fife Ness were stunning. Our soundtrack was from a

Scottish composer, Arthur Johnston, a friend of Andrew's. I felt I was seeing around the corner, but filmmaking was such an unholy process compared to painting, I felt.

On this stay in London, I wanted to see some contemporary French films, then shown at the Academy Cinema in Oxford Street. I was a bit early, and rather than walk along busy Oxford Street, I turned down a lane running parallel to it. The backs of the shops presented black doors to the damp lane, and the noise of the traffic hummed away in the background. Ahead of me, I saw a strange-looking motorcycle awkwardly leaning against one of these doorways. It looked abandoned, but what a motorcycle it was. It was an old Brough Superior SS 100. Somebody had spilled paint over its cut-down mudguards, and it looked completely trashed. *Did somebody steal it*? I wondered. The carburettor was dismantled and the float chamber was missing. *Was it abandoned, or was some poor biker trying his hardest to get it moving so he could get home?*

I wander about and think, *I could have that old machine on the train to Scotland simply by pushing it along to Euston Station.* In Scotland, I had a road tax registration book for a Brough Superior registration number BFS 101. I did a project on Broughs some time before. Like all my projects, I had two examples of the bike and Christmas treed them so I only needed one registration book (CS 6029).

It seemed futile, but I do futile things like knock on the back doors of stores to see whether anyone knows anything about the bike. There's no answer. The lane is deserted. I look again and again at the bike, and it looks abandoned and uncared for. I could rebuild it to its former glory. *But hold on! I just did all that, and surely I'm past all that now. I'm making films at the RCA and painting new ideas at Fife Ness. I should be putting childish things behind me, shouldn't I?* How strange this connection to my imagination: a machine with a past.

I circle about, my head filled with possibilities. I think, *I am going to dream and fill the ends of books with images of getting this motorcycle to Lundin Links in future years. But no! I must grow up and get on with new ideas!*

Slowly, I walk along Oxford Street and go to the pictures. To think that, in 2008, I wrote, "I'm 70 years old, and I'm talking to a motorcycle." Nothing ever seems to change. What doors was I hoping to open with those uncanny machines?

In a film, *The Painter's Landscape,* I desperately wanted to make connections between what the artist made and what the artist saw. I was looking and looking, seeing and seeing. The big question for the young artist is, "Do you want to look through an already-open door, or do you want a door to open a door to yourself."

In Scotland, this was never an issue. It was assumed that the already-open door was a good bargain for anybody and everybody and likely to be much more successful. Especially during the art-student years and the years following them. But there seems to be a time when this call for adventure, as Saint-Exupéry says, "moves you, torments you as it does all men. Whether we call it sacrifice, poetry, or adventure the voice is the same."

In 2008, I looked back at Fife Ness, Lilliput, and Pictish Stones and those first, faltering steps to making a film. It was a long way from *The Naked Pilot* ... or was it? I remember there was a spate of films, art films, in the sixties. The artist looked at a subject and, lo and behold, a painting appeared. It was as simple as that. Something had to be done about the seeing, the image-making, the connections, the artists' relationships with their subjects. In my case, a sense of being a stranger, an outsider, in this simple equation. This search was to last a long time.

I remember some of the phrases: "Find something outside Scottish art"; "The stones speak of it, the standing stones of Scotland"; "This art is an enigma." All this carried on for a long time.

The film was shown at the Edinburgh Film Festival in 1967, forty years before *Ruchenlage* (*Upside down*), and it was a great help in my teaching career. It took me all the way up to Aberdeen College of Education for an interview for an exciting job. I remember taking up all these paintings from Fife Ness and the film for the interview and meeting Jimmy Scotland and Bill Burns for the first time. I got the job, and as they say, I never looked back.

In Aberdeen, we opened a door in art education. Bill Burns, an ex-fighter pilot of the Second World War, put together a new idea for teacher training in 1966 when graduates had to spend three full terms in teacher training. His new idea was *area investigation.*

For the famous teaching practice, the students were sent to the far outposts of our catchment area where they spent three weeks. This time, however, they would focus on their connection to teaching. The painters would paint, the sculptors would sculpt, and the printmakers, textile designers, and graphic designers would investigate their area, their people, and society. Their findings would be exhibited in the classrooms of Orkney, Shetland, the Hebrides, and The north-east of Scotland. From these bountiful, fresh visual connections, new ideas exploded in the classroom, providing new subjects for children of all ages and a fresh insight into the whole process of visual education.

A novel such as A J Cronin's *Stars Look Down* would be used by other departments within the college as a project to help make connections in art, music, English, and education. New staff was appointed to follow through and connections and cooperation flourished. And what a scheme! I remember so well my first visit to Orkney, to Shetland, and to the Hebrides. My pilot's licence seemed part of the idea and gave the area investigation an even greater dimension. The students were thrilled to travel and take part where their skills and insights played such an impactful part of the latest thing in art education.

Gwen and Amy's Premonitions

The weather gets more and more wintry and the light fades. My daughter, Gwen, comes over from New York, and off we go to the borders and Deepsykehead Farm. My elder daughter lives there with her husband and three children. She is completing the most amazing film documentary of her life, *The Edge of Dreaming.*

"What do you think of premonitions," we are asked by Amy. Amy had had two premonitions, both dangerous. The first was about her horse called George. In a dream, he came up to Amy, looked at her, fell to one side, and died. At 2:00 a.m., Amy awoke, got up, went outside, and found George dead on his side.

The second premonition was more complicated. Her first husband, Arthur, a filmmaker who had died some years before, appeared in another dream. This time, the message was more dangerous. He told Amy she would not live to see her next birthday. The film, *The Edge of Dreaming,* is the story of Amy's subsequent illness and her attempts to survive the premonition of her own death.

To document such drastic happenings seems to need a kind of transparency in the family creating a visual focus on the light, the texture, the body language and the words of all of us against the background of Deepsykehead. The camera picks up such messages. The documentary format is so honest and revealing, I am filled with admiration in regards to the editing and selection of such a heart-of-the-matter trial of the imagination.

Amy held a birthday party in 2007 and celebrated her escape as the day dawned and she was still alive. She had her family and friends around her at Deepsykehead, and the bonfire and Chinese dragon indicated a celebration that nobody would forget. She went on filming, and over the years, she built up a remarkable film about the years from her mother's death in 1999 to the present.

Our response to Amy's question – "What do you think of premonitions?" – is interesting and revealing. My own response is instant sympathy and a kind of resignation to premonitions that won't go away. My advice to Amy is to talk to people.

When Peter Forbes asked me to take his aeroplanes down to Leeds/Bradford for servicing, it meant starting very early from Aberdeen, flying to Leeds, waiting all day for the aeroplane to be serviced, and then flying it back to Aberdeen. It would mean a long day exposed to the weather. This kind of stretching of one's abilities produced anxiety in me, which certainly makes for premonitions, especially when the weather starts poorly and one has to travel to the aerodrome from one's warm bed very early in the morning. It helped to expose my sensibilities to the weather as soon as possible. I travelled to the aerodrome on an old, vintage motorbike, enacted a physical response to the weather, and took nothing for granted. *Would the old machine start? Would it run well enough?* Perhaps all this gave me an alternative anxiety that the human psyche is good enough to make a place for. The wetter and colder it was on the motorbike, the more I kept the flight in perspective. My senses became more and more heightened, and as I rode the bike from Kemnay to Dyce, I could smell perfume and damp clothes on the people waiting at bus stops. My eyesight seemed sharpened by adrenalin, and the various stages of anxiety and fear were contained in my mini trial before the main trial of the flight.

I arrived at Dyce, parked the vintage bike carefully, and opened the hangar doors to get the aeroplane ready for the opening of the aerodrome. Mine was the first flight at 7:00 a.m. I loved pulling out the Rupert-type aeroplane, and saw it all as a kind of Rupert and Nutwood adventure. The repeated checks, the familiarity of maps and flight plans, and eventually, talking to the airfield controller. It all gave me a wonderful reassurance, especially if the weather behaved as forecast and the clouds and visibility improved and things began to look good. The premonitions fade as the engine starts. I continue feeling the motorbike and the raw sense of the early morning coolness and start of the day. *Is this all in the imagination?* I muse.

I would have loved to talk to Saint-Exupéry, Bill Burns, and Amy Johnson about premonitions, but it is the kind of subject that is written up afterwards, often by other people. Guesses are made about remarks in conversations and letters. Perhaps one doesn't want to talk about premonitions directly. I know my daughter had to go to great lengths to deal with hers. Scientists describe the brain and the senses wonderfully. I liked the remark in her film that the poor human brain was limited to only five senses. One scientist felt there was another one or two struggling to get out, and perhaps that was what was causing all the trouble!

The shamans that Amy consulted stated categorically that it was impossible to contact any kind of extraterrestrial energy if there was fear. Once without fear, the imagination can find a dialogue that can help our paltry five senses and give us forms and images to match our nightmares and awful warnings.

Talking and connections are paramount once again; survival takes a lot of practice, doesn't it! "*C'est un peu, Mozart assassine*" – we all have to keep this idea of Mozart moving throughout all of us via our own imaginative energy more directly than we first thought. We need more naked pilots.

Naked Pilot (after El Greco) James Hardie, 1999

"This call moved you; it torments you as it does all men. Whether we call it sacrifice, poetry, or adventure the voice is the same. The tame duck had no idea its head was vast enough to contain oceans, continents and skies; but there it is, beating its wings, refusing the grain and the worms. 'The call of the wild' – the wild ducks fly over in curving arrowheads on their continent-spanning migrations," said Saint-Exupéry.

Hogmanay in 2008

At Hogmanay, Gwen and I are in Carlops for the celebrations. Angus McNicol and Gerda Stevenson introduce us to Andrew Greig, a fascinating writer on these dimensions of the imagination that so enthral the Hardies at this very time. Books such as *The Return of John McNab; When They Lay Bare* and *That Summer* make enthralling connections to the naked pilots among us. I read *That Summer* in 2006. On the title page of the book, I wrote, "This summer chilling out at Deepsykehead to GBSMD Nord 1101 1947 26/6/06."

I was flying the Nord and finding it difficult. I was really stretched practically and imaginatively. Dreams come true, but there is a price that must be paid. I felt these two sides – the practical and the imaginative – strongly. I felt almost haunted by the focus on the aeroplane and the pilot.

That Summer by Andrew Greig focused on the summer of 1940, when The Battle of Britain occurred. He invents two characters, Len Westbourne, a pilot, and Stella Gardam, a radar operator. Through them, he tells the story of their generation caught up in that summer of the Second World War.

The summer of 2006 is warm, and on a hot day in June, I am left on my own at Deepsykehead to read Andrew Greig's book. I read it all at one go, moving about the farm and eventually finding an inflatable boat on a lochan. My fragile imagination soaks up the story of Len and Stella. I am on my back in the boat under the blue sky and the dragonflies, and I am left alone by midges and flies. The boat drifts in the wind and nudges itself round reeds, rocks, and the banks of the lochan. Deepsykehead is the place to really read a book. Through the book, my connections to the RAF are remembered and fulfilled in this unusual setting of the Scottish Borders. I remember the atmosphere of the wartime RAF Station and the smells of the landscape. I remember the damp, chill mornings; I remember, as a child, a kiltie, some chocolate, and cigarette smoke mixed with the intoxicating smells of dung, dampness, and frost.

On the title page of *Last Summer,* the inscription reads, "Dad died 14 July 2006 to the vanishing generation." I'm reminded of my memorial flight on 13 August 2006.

My suffering imagination pushed the idea of flying a vintage aeroplane into a memorial flight to my father, and it was this practical feel of the controls, this sensation of flying (courtesy of the Wright brothers) that helped my imagination key a goodbye to a vanishing generation in August. That was about four weeks after the funeral of "Dad" in St Andrews on another gin-clear day with a light on Scotland that I will always remember. The whole Sunday morning was stopped in time, and there seemed to be no noise left.

My generation tried hard to connect to the generation of the war. My friend, Bobby McGregor, brought war books home from Larkhall Public Library all his life. He read and reread those classics that became so outdated as the propaganda faded and so many anti-hero versions came out. Bobby died in 2003, and his daughter, Fiona, asked me whether I wanted his war book collection. I had the same collection and didn't have room for any more. The more one read, the more difficult it was to connect to the experience of the generation that had produced us. I find out now, in 2006, that these connections have to be paid for and developed by commitment both practical and imaginative. How difficult it is to understand all this, to see it clearly. It takes so much time and experience. But the aeroplane has helped.

"Son's Memorial Flight to Honour His Father"

St Andrew's Citizen, 25 August 2006

His generation is disappearing, and as the Scottish writer Andrew Greig said, "A vanishing generation, whose code was sacrifice and whose quest was a decent normality, though it was one that had never quite existed. Who were so baffled by our turning away from what they had made."

Gwen and I walk along the main road at Carlops in the Hogmanay Torchlight Procession, we hear the church bell ring, and we watch the balloons fly off into the dark, starry sky. After a glass of mulled wine, it's off to the Ceilidh in the Village Hall. Sally Charlton, Amy's old friend, gets us dancing, and in the Canadian barn dance, I dance with every beautiful woman in Carlops Hall! They do things so well in the Borders. Goodbye, 2008.

Journeys of 2009

LE Velocette and "Hangar" Skelmorlie, 2009

The first journeys of 2009 are very silvery. The weather turns mild but cloudy with that variant density of vapour that has a silver tinsel quality to it. Showers have a grey density about them, and cotton wools creep about but don't spoil the silver for too long.

I pull out the LE Velo to run over to Deepsykehead in the Borders. I can avoid motorways and find roads where the wind is always at my back – a good place to be when you've only 8 bhp. I remind myself that Wilbur Wright only had 10 bhp when his valves got hot. Cool, man, cool.

The Velo mustn't be hurried; too much throttle and there seems to be a rich cut again, more familiar to aeroplane engines than motorcycles. Forty mph seems satisfactory, and the light-engine burbles its way up hill and down dale very smoothly. Its 80 mi to Deepsykehead, and the wind is from the south-west. Lunch at Newmilns, and it takes *only* three and half hours to get to the farm.

The leg shields stop the cramps, and the fifties style creates a connection to Kilmarnock, Galston; Newmilns; Darvel; Drumclog; Louden Hill; Strathhaven; Kirkmuirhill; Hazlebank; Kirkfieldbank; Lanark; Carstairs; Carnwarth; Elsrickle; Dolphinton; West Linton; Carlops and Deepsykehead.

I remember bicycling to Hazlebank from Larkhall with the pannier bag filled with school books. The Highers of 1955 were conquered reading on a bench beside the Clyde at Hazlebank. Why was weather so much better then than now?

My other journey is to see my old aeroplane, still abandoned at West Connel, near Oban. I have to wish her a happy new year. The Sunday is forecast is dry. What a route: Sandpoint to Hunters Quay; Coylet; Whistlefield; Strachur; Creggans; Cairndow; Inverary; Cladich; Lochawe; Pass of Brander; Bonawe, and finally Ledaig North Connel.

No more 8 bhp; now I have a 440 cc Veetwin, which probably develops about 48 bhp, even when the valves get hot. This fast bike is related to my Veetwin projects of Brough Superiors and Vincent HRDs. I've been a lucky motorcyclist! My Honda Bros makes this silver journey of corners, glens, and lochside roads a thing of inspiration, a fitting dedication to the aeroplane that rests in its hangar at North Connel.

The new engine for the Nord is installed, but not yet with carburettors and exhaust pipes. Jim Fergusson comes up the road with me on his Honda Fireblade, and we have soup and bacon rolls in the gliding clubroom at North Connel. There, I meet someone who connects to Bill Burns when they both taught in Dunoon. We talk about Bill and his area investigation idea, which feels somehow appropriate on this unusual aerodrome.

I remember making a flight in March 1980 for Bill Burns' area investigation at Aberdeen College of Education. I was to fly from Aberdeen to Glenforsa on Mull and tutor two art students at Tobermoray Academy. My colleague from Aberdeen, Frank Pottinger, was to be dropped at North Connel for Oban High School for the same purpose. I would pick him up a day or two later at North Connel.

The weather deteriorated – not silvery, more like lead. And it's heavy and windy. The morning of departure, I got down from Tobermoray early to a deserted Glenforsa airstrip and tried to make a decision as to whether I should take off and fly over to North Connel to pick up Frank who would be waiting there.

So much has happened since those days in the seventies. I was to learn a great deal at this "High Noon at Glenforsa."

The previous summer, I had a flying lesson that made all the difference. The flying instructor was Wendy Craik. I was introduced to Wendy by the bold Peter Forbes at Pegasus Flying Aberdeen. First impressions were not good: she was all high heels and painted fingernails. She had pilot boyfriends for the day shift and the night shift. Still, she was the best flying instructor I ever met.

"Never been north of Watford Gap in *me* life, big boy," was her opening gambit, but we flew down to Strathallan airstrip near Auchterarder, and she took stock of my flying. She had changed completely in the aeroplane and become a highly professional pilot who asked what kind of flying I was meaning to do. On hearing of area investigations and adventures in the Highlands, she decided to do a survival course for happy-go-lucky pilots like myself. She told me about the Fowler flaps on the Cessna 152: "Put full flaps down and take off," said Wendy. This was on the grass at Strathallan. "But you can't do that," said the naked pilot. "Really, try it anyway." With full flaps, the Cessna rears into the air at about 40 knot. From there, one can climb away, raising the enormous flaps gradually as the aeroplane lifts off the ground. Wow! We practised some short landings and cloud avoidance. I was very impressed with Wendy.

So back to High Noon at Glenforsa; I walked up and down the grass strip. The wind from the west divided round Ben More and gusted in various directions. It was raining, and puddles had formed all over the grass strip. Last night in Tobermoray, the BBC forecast winds of 45 knots. In the winter, the north of Scotland seems deserted – there's nobody around to chat things over. I walk the course noting the track through the soggy grass and the large puddles. I felt it could be done, I could get into the air and fly over to North Connel. North Connel was an old, wartime tarmac runway of some 1,200 yards compared to Glenforsa's wet grass of 750 yards.

I start up and do all my checks. In the shelter of Ben More, it doesn't seem too bad. With full power and as the plane gathers speed, I steer between the puddles. After a clear patch, it looks good. But suddenly, a gust sends the little Cessna turning like a weathercock. Everything then goes wrong: a wheel catches a puddle, and I know that if I try to correct and pull it out, the next gust is going to blow the plane over.

So I do a Wendy: the electric flaps switch down, and suddenly the aeroplane rears to about twenty feet. I put the stick hard forward, and I let the crosswind gusts take me over the fence and over the sea. Thank you, Wendy Craik.

Easing up the flaps, the Cessna stabilises and trims out at 70 knots. The area investigation is saved for another day. The landing at North Connel is so much easier on a tarmac with a fairly straightforward headwind. I must see *High Noon* again.

North Connel Oban and the New Engine

North Connel Oban

At last, I'm looking through the windscreen of an aeroplane. I have my flying shoes on, and I am sitting on my lambskin fleece. The cockpit is cold, damp, and somehow unfamiliar. It's 2009 and time to recover the aeroplane and fly it back to Prestwick. We've crack-tested all the components, especially the all-alloy connecting rods. Every particle of corrosion has been removed and treated. It's all bolted together and hanging upside down in its cradle in MDelta. We're outside the gliding hangar at North Connel, and this is the test of two engineers to see that everything has been put back and is joined up to the right connections. I push the throttle open and close it back; push and close; push and close, same with the mixture; rich and weak, rich and weak. The track of the cables has to be seen to be unhindered. Push and close, push and close. rich and weak, just like life, or as they say, "*Cho coltach ri, beatha duine*!"

There is the ritual of filling the compressed air cylinder in the aeroplane from the cylinder carted all the way up to Oban. First of all, the external supply has to have a fragile-looking brass adapter that bolts on to the heavy air cylinder, which is coloured black. There's a zip as the valve is opened and the dial inside MDelta slowly rises to a red line, marking the safety valve limit that frightens everybody as it blows. We now have over 20 HPZ pressure – enough for a cold start.

I sit in the aeroplane. Adnan and Dave have the fire extinguishers at the ready, so I say, "Clear the prop" and make sure the magnets are on. I open the valve and hear a feeble sound as the air escapes before we can get it to the starter. That means there are leaks!

Back to the filling ritual; "Clear the prop," I say, but there is no joy. The Viet starter has to be timed to the firing sequence and has its own little valve in each cylinder. Back to the drawing board! The afternoon darkens and snow drifts in from Mull and the Sound. We dance the wingtip-less, old aeroplane back into the hangar and pack up for the day.

Is this time of no flying aeroplane going to be a limbo of frustration, or is it going to be a time for recharging the batteries? I wonder.

Looking through the windscreen of an aeroplane on the ground reminds me of Chicago. I did my American flying licence at Midway Airport, which is right in the middle of the city of Chicago. It's the biggest airport I've ever flown from. The flying club was miles from the runways and needed directions from a handheld map to negotiate. I always seemed to get lost on the flat prairie of space and had to ask for "a progression" either to or from the flying club. It felt dangerous to cross runways left and right, and I felt I needed the ATC on the ground more than in the air!

In 1989, I had become an exchange tutor at the School of the Art Institute of Chicago. It's located in the Midwest of the United States. I was curious to see art and flying out and away from Europe, it was easy to fall into a kind of limbo between the urgent familiarity of Scotland and the vastness of the prairie space in the Midwest. I had great sympathy for the black student in my life drawing class who drew his preliminary stick figure not in the corner of his sheet of paper, but right in the very middle of the sheet. He then drew his life drawing to fill the sheet, leaving a feeling of identity in the small, voodoo-like stick figure. I got him to make 3D figures as well as drawings, and I began to wonder myself just what was going on. Whatever it was, the fear of the vacuum seems to count a lot over there. Does it have something to do with the wide open prairies or the disorientation of artificial studios of art? I would have loved to hold the door open a little longer.

I shared a studio complex with four active American artists in Chicago. On my days off from teaching, I worked hard at my painting for a one-man show about halfway through the semester.

There was an intensity in the work that I had noticed in the life drawing. I shared the studio complex with a sculptor who made full-sized figures with a strange presence. He would then make the bottom half of the figure male and the top half female. These figures would be moved all round the building. The last artist to leave locked up and put the lights out. That artist was often me, and as I moved along the dark corridor to the front door, I often saw gleaming red lights that I hoped were fire extinguisher lights and not cigarette ends. These tiny lights were just strong enough to let me glimpse a pair of breasts gleaming over a penis – all on the same figure, I might add. I closed the door quietly and went out into the warm Chicago night hoping the car I had parked was still there to be used for the getaway.

Flying in North America can be strange. The squared fields repeat and repeat as the miles are covered. Small aerodromes were fully automated, and one could land and depart wholly on the Automatic Transmission Information Service (ATIS). There was always a temptation to fly and fly until I came to a river such as the Mississippi before turning round and returning to the same square fields and straight roads.

Recovery of Nord from North Connel

I open the throttle, and with a roar of mechanical ecstasy, the aeroplane bounds down the runway. I ease the nosewheel up at 40 and break the bounds of earth at 50 knots. A beautiful day at North Connel March is doing its best for us, and silvery spring is beginning to get some colour. Even the sea is starting to glitter. The somewhat-familiar instrument panel looks back at me as my eyes keep track of the instruments. The air-speed indicator is chief; the ball in the middle, Wilbur, keeps his eye on us; the altimeter with its barometric setting its QNH (height above sea level) and QFE (field elevation) puts it all together. There are wonderful sensations through the joystick as the speeding air gives it muscled flight after six months of hangarage. Six months of standing still, of looking through cockpit windows gathering dust and bird droppings. It's not easy to recharge the batteries when the aeroplane becomes earthbound for so long. Motorcycles, aeroplanes, and art – there's no getting away from them. Is it a witch's brew or dynamic connections for insight into life's mysteries? Who knows?

I get an image of Vincenzo Lunardi and his balloon. "A flying mortal," he felt himself mirrored in the faces of Edinburgh and Glasgow in 1785. He loved the attention, the slightly frozen looks that follow the movements of the aeronaut even though they are not sharing the adventure. I liked his toast "Lunardi, the favourite of the ladies."

Sunday at North Connel in the twenty-first century -the Sabbath in Scotland. In the early morning, we leave Prestwick and drive north to recover the Nord. Splendid motorways, especially when empty at this time on a Sunday. Over the Erskine Bridge and up Loch Lomondside to Crianlarich. It's going to take some time as we motor steadily, earthbound on an aerial adventure.

In 1956, I remember the same feeling of expectation on the same road. My father had persuaded me to ride pillion on a motorcycle and camp for a week at Cape Wrath in the north-west of Scotland. Our adventure was to cross the Sound of Durness with the motorcycle and ride the 11 mi of track to the lighthouse at Cape Wrath. The motorbike would be pushed onto a rowing boat. Somebody held the bike upright as we sailed over the sea to Cape Wrath. I remember my father buying whiskies in the local hotel bar for the worthy boatmen who seemed to have cousins and second cousins appear as the gentleman dug deep into his motorcycling coat pockets. Expectations were fulfilled all round.

We drive on to Bonawe. There has been a fatal accident on Loch Awe. We've heard that three men have been lost in a late-night fog returning from the pub to their campsite across the loch. Boating, like flying, is totally ruled by the weather. Fog just makes confusion rule, and even Vincenzo Lunardi and Wilbur Wright can do nothing but give in to nature's sleight of hand. This fine morning, nature is gentle and sly, waiting for the next innocents.

Sunday at North Connel, we open the gliding hangar and Declan Curtis's face is a picture as he sees the continental beauty in her Luftwaffe finery for the first time in six months.

I plant a kiss on her cold cheek and wonder what she has in store for the two innocents who remove her covers and push her out into the sunlight. I like the way aeroplanes move on their long legs and fat tyres. The weight is high, the movement jaunty and cavalier compared to the deadweight of a motorbike or car. The Nord shares her winter hangar with a Slingsby motorglider with a wingspan of 40 ft, which is pushed out on a trolley and shivers nervously in the open air.

Adnan, Declan, and I start to get the Nord ready for flight. We start with the engine. This enormous upside down engine bears no resemblance to the Pope Toledo of the Wright brothers or the Velocette LE flat twin. It reminds me of the engines of the Second World War. Being upside down, the crankshaft brings the propeller to a high position with more ground clearance for the propeller and a better power line for the airframe. The older aeroplanes like the Gypsy Moth always seem to lead with their chin, and the upright cylinders and exhaust pipes stick up above the crankshaft.

The engine is going through a tremendous amount of oil, and we're not having much success with the new rings on the old pistons. Seemingly, the Renault 6Q10 has steel piston rings that are difficult to bed in with the steel cylinder barrels. So the blow past is causing tremendous crankcase pressures, and oil is bursting out all over, just like spring. Do we run it in or start again with a different honing of the bores in the cylinder? Deltair did the cylinder heads, bores, and pistons, but they suggest bringing the engine down to a testbed and trying again.

VinTec rebuilt a Renault 6Q for a German client with seemingly good results. Half a litre of oil burnt per hour compared to my three to four litres per hour. I start the engine and warm up the oil. She runs ragged at first, but she settles down after a bit and the oil pressure looks good. It's a cool morning, and the oil temperature takes its time coming up the dial. The vacuum is working, and I turn on the three valves to *ouvert*. The hydraulic dial seems to be stuck at 50 g/cm It's been sitting such a long time.

The three of us look at each other, and there's an urgency to get going. Wingtips and radio aerial! I help with the wingtips, and Declan does the radio aerial. The wingtip bolts are different for the starboard fitting and port fitting, and the forward bolt passes through three thicknesses of metal. The ever-present silver gas-tape seals the two gaps and we have wings! The Nord's no longer clipped, clapped, and cropped. It's high noon at North Connel!

As I taxi round to apron C for the petrol bowser, I think of Vincenzo Lunardi. There's a Sunday crowd at the gliding club, and they feel very involved in the recovery of our balloon. The Nord's been in their hangar since September 2008, and it's now 29 March 2009. We've a date with the petrol bowser at 1:00 p.m., and I taxi over to apron C and park next to the Islander who's flying off to Coll and Colonsay.

The four petrol tanks on the Nord are connected up with small-bore pipes and are slow filling. I keep the fuel brimming on the lip of the petrol cap, and we take some 90 litres of fresh fuel. Her heart is full and brimming over! We now start up and do our checks very seriously. The Ratier propeller has been fitted with a new relay box and power is getting to the coarse/fine mechanism. The test is to put the command switch to manual. The Toggle-switch is moved to the right for *coarse.* As the propeller pitch coarsens, the revs fall on the rev-counter. Switch left to *fine,* and the revs rise again. The red and green lights aren't coming on, but the revs show its working. Back to *coarse,* and the revs fall again. The command lever is pushed down to *automatic,* but there's no rise in revs. Still, we have control over the pitch, and we can make sure we have the adjustment we need for take-off, cruising, and landing.

There's still no rise in hydraulic pressure, and the indicator is stuck on 50 g when it should rise to about 120 g. Adnan checks there's pressure in the pipe, but there's no way of proving it as there's no demand on the hydraulics other than the undercarriage. *Will we be able to raise and lower the undercarriage?* I wonder.

We decide we can fly to Prestwick with the undercarriage down, and I have checked the emergency operation of the air pressure to the nose wheel. I checked this in my garage and was impressed with the separate emergency reservoir of pressure in the air tank. I check the air pressure and build this up by turning on the generator in the aeroplane.

Nord 1101 GBSMD, 1947

High noon at North Connel or bad day at Blackrock? We do our radio checks, and we have strength four and five. The radio sounds fine, and Declan has his handheld radio and his GPS, so we think we are ready.

In the left-hand seat, I have the throttle and the brakes. I line up on runway 19. Using the full length of the runway, the engine seems smoother. Our ground revs are better than the old engine. I open the throttle, and the roar of ecstasy comes from the plane and the pilots.

We raise the undercarriage at the end of the runway, but we can't get the red lights for up. We try again, but we put the undercarriage to down and climb slowly to orbit the field. We have greens for the main undercarriage, but none for the nose wheel! We decide to fly to Prestwick with the undercarriage down. We know it'll take us about fifty minutes given the headwind.

Out of the corner of my eye, I saw some black smoke, and we ask the North Connel tower to give us some visual checking. They report some smoke and confirm our undercarriage is down. The smoke goes, though, and I feel the engine is pulling healthily, so the decision is to go on to Prestwick in our state. The weather is good; there's a front just coming in from the west, and we can see Mull disappearing in the rain, but Prestwick's weather is good with a handy wind on runway 21 of about 15 knots at 200. I let MD climb to above 2,000, and we fly, ball in the middle, down to the Crinan Canal.

With the undercarriage down, we are blown a bit north and arrive over Rothesay on the Isle of Bute. We turn south to the Ayrshire coast and report our position to the helpful Prestwick Control and enter controlled airspace near Ardrossan. A Sea King rescue helicopter nurses us along as it approaches Prestwick. Now for the big moment: Declan pushes the emergency red lever.

We can't hear the whoosh over the noise of the engine, but lo and behold, the green light shines bright and the nose wheel is locked down. Everyone in the cockpit sighs with relief. The ball stays in the middle, Wilbur, and here's to Vincenzo, the favourite of the ladies! A rather daunting sign on the instrument panel informs us that the last check on the undercarriage is hydraulic pressure. We have none. Declan is full of ideas and in his element. He approaches high and asks for right base on runway 21 wind 200 / 15 knots. With lots of power, we must keep that nose wheel high. We touch down on the main wheels at 55 knots and keep the nose wheel high as long as possible. Against the wind, the Nord slows quickly and we don't touch the brakes. Will we be able to taxi back to the flying club apron at the control tower? Gently, I press the starboard brake, and we turn right into whisky and slowly taxi back green lights steady and bright.

We heave a sigh of relief as we open the doors into the March sunlight. The fire service van stops beside us and asks how we are. Our faces must tell him all he needs to know. Declan is like Red Rum. Red Rum is only Red Rum because of the challenge of the Grand National and all his wins at Aintree. The challenge of flying this old, vintage aeroplane gives Declan the same kind of proof of the right stuff as Aintree gave Red Rum.

The ball in the middle slides to one side as the vacuum is switched off and the instruments run down. Silence descends on the old mechanisms connecting us to the thirties and forties. One old aeroplane one; an old artist and Red Rum – not a bad image from fifty minutes of flying. Are the faces at North Connel still looking at the sky? What happened to Vincenzo Lunardi after his challenges of 1785 and the adoration of the ladies of Edinburgh? Perhaps the strangest thing in flying is that nothing at all happens after the aeroplane is shut down; after all those moments of crisis and adventure, nothing exists at all. The crowd goes home, the big top is lowered, and all that's left are a few marks in the grass. The next shower of rain covers them up, and we all wait for the sun to shine again.

"Over empty lands and salt seas."

Isle of Arran in 2009

The noise seemed unconnected to anything: *Whump, whump, whump,* with a kind of compressed air urgency about it. Not an aeroplane. I was lying on a beach near Corrie on the Isle of Arran. My twisted ankle ached, and I was giving it the sea treatment. Salt, iodine, and nitrogen for free. And then I saw the two wild swans. The *whump, whump* became more urgent and very slowly, the first swan got airborne, followed by his mate. They inched upwards and upwards until they were about five feet above the calm sea. They were taking off into wind, and I was reminded me of last Sunday's drama at North Connel.

The swans' undercarriage dragged a bit as it had been used for furious paddling to help them take off. But what an image to get off from the sea and make it look so difficult! What muscular stamina to keep up that rate of flying. It reminded me, too, that the Nord 1101's Air Force name was *Ramier* or *wild pigeon.* There's something about the breast of the swan and the pigeon that is so feminine and streamlined. Magnificent! Vincenzo Lunardi would agree!

My ankle aches a bit because, a fortnight ago, I sprained it while sliding down a steep reservoir bank. I still don't know what happened. I think my mind was on the aeroplane when I zigzagged to disaster. My brother, Tom, invited me over to Arran where he hired a cottage for a few days. I don't think I'm going to be much good at walking the hills of Arran, so it's back to my 8 bhp Wright Flyer Velocette.

The swans decide for me. I'll ride right round the Island to see whether I can hold on to my bigger picture. My dialogue with Wilbur and Vincent can't do my ankle any harm, and the weather has the sun in it at last.

Le Velo runs well. No more oiled plugs, rich cuts, ice in the carburettors. She runs well in her three gears. Her 8 bhp, small clutch and shaft drive designed in 1948 have a quality and charm for the narrow, twisty roads of Arran. The road surfaces test out the suspension, especially on hairpins and bridges. Here and there, newly surfaced roads give the old bike a break, and we fly along with scarce a hiccup. I find it quite difficult to ride with its slow hand-change and get caught on some sudden, steep turns up the hills and glens. Coming to a halt on a steep hill is not to be recommended, and it's difficult to restart. The clutch objects to this treatment and slips and vibrates. This is not good and could lead to the oil seal giving up again. It's a vintage technique that's needed. I sit tall in the saddle and think about motorcycling. It's like that notice in the flying club: "Are you flying the aeroplane you think you're flying?"

It's a real break from the Nord and its recovery. A more light-hearted, summer day feel to the whole operation. The air off the Atlantic is fresh, but real oxygen seems to get through to man and machine. In April in Arran, the daffodils and the broom seem further on than the mainland hardly 14 mi away. Is it the Gulf Stream again that's making a practice Brigadoon out of bonnie Scotland?

If only one could pick such a day for flying in the last thirty years. I've hardly been aloft in this perfect gin-clear weather, particularly when it's important to fly and complete some idea or exercise.

I remember 4 July 2007. This was an American/Scottish ceremony to celebrate the bicentenary of the birth of the great Scottish engineer, Thomas Telford. The film we had just managed to make and edit would be shown to this august body with a gallus fly-past by the Nord. This was my first commission with the plane, and I could see all this in my dreams. The ceremony was at Craigellachie Bridge, but as the day dawned, the weather forecast was appalling. A front lay across the north of Scotland from Aberdeen to Inverness, right across the River Spey and Craigellachie. I was standing by from 5:00 a.m. Weather was not too bad in Prestwick, but a phone call to Lossiemouth Met put the whole flight out of the question. Even the RAF was not flying that morning. All these sad phone calls were made, and my fly-past was cancelled. All these hopeful arrangements and publicity, there's just no arguing with the weather gods.

When things go wrong, it's difficult to keep up the bigger picture. Stress and strain – there's nothing like them for pushing down our ability to hold on to the vision, the idealism that starts our projects. It's the classic downward path. In comes self-pity and a kind of narrow focus, a kind of barrenness that is difficult to remove from the psyche. More mistakes lead to more mistakes. I'm surprised at my language as I make mistakes on the old Velo or thud into another Arran pothole and rick my back on the old suspension. There's a dynamic to all this: the next project or work can often pick up the bigger picture with a kind of leap over quality, leap over the level of the stressed-out failure.

It's a bit like Saint-Exupéry's *The Little Prince* coming after the fall of France and the numbing experiences of surrender and defeat. Saint-Exupéry's bigger picture was a strange tale, a fable using space and planet. What a wonderful vision of reconciliation of dreams and anguish.

"The important thing," as he wrote in *Flight to Arras,* "is not exaltation. There is no hope of exaltation in defeat. The important thing is to get dressed, to climb aboard and to take off. What we may think of it ourselves is of no importance. The child who would derive a sense of exaltation from grammar lessons would strike me as suspect and pretentious. The important thing is to conduct oneself with reference to a goal which is not immediately visible."

The Bigger Picture

LE Velocette and Nord 1101 Prestwick, 2009

I left Fetternear in Aberdeenshire in 1980 and came down south. I came down to a new job in the Glasgow School of Art looking for a bigger picture. Not just in motorcycles and aeroplanes, but in art, that small word of three letters that has haunted me all my life. I had always felt strongly about the act of art and the first-hand experience of using brushes, colour, paint, palette knives, sticks, Polyfilla, sand, and other related items.

I had tried to connect my experiences, sensations, and images in as powerful a way as I possibly could. Fife, Aberdeenshire, and Ayrshire were the moves I made, but what doors would open?

Interviews at colleges are slightly unreal experiences. In Aberdeen College of Education, I met such exotics as Bill Burns, Jimmy Scotland, Gerald Osborne, and Roy Stark. In the interview, they sat in a variety of positions, almost like in a play, and plied me with questions. I had brought a van full of my own paintings as well as my collection of paintings for children from the Fife schools I had worked in. The new degree (B. Ed.) meant that I could be made a member of the university court based on the outcome of this interview alone!

Gerald Osborne sat with his feet on his desk, immediately giving the impression of Oxbridge and "Goals that were not immediately visible." Jimmy Scotland, the principal, was very witty and interesting, and he created a bigger picture out of his passion for drama and Shakespeare and education. Bill Burns, the head of the art department, was impressed by my film *The Painter's Landscape* and my struggle to connect and make images. It was a great experience, particularly when they offered me the job. I was lucky to join Aberdeen College of Education in 1968.

By comparison, the interview at Glasgow School of Art felt like more of the same. David Donaldson and Geoff Squires had been tutors of mine in the fifties, and Jimmy Robertson and Dougal Cameron had been there all their working lives. It seemed a small, unchanging world at 167 Renfrew Street, but changes were in the air! Sandy Moffat was a new face for me. In 1985, Sandy wrote: "Why should such a concentration of vital, young painters suddenly burst forth in Glasgow, a city where, for the last quarter century, the visual arts have appeared backward looking and parochial?

It should be remembered that there was always a strong tradition of figurative and expressive painting in Glasgow (Colquoun; MacBryde; Eardley and Crozier), but all that survived of this tradition had become, by the late seventies, lifeless and respectable, destroyed by an admixture of middle-class taste and banal abstraction. (Bruce McLean fled in 1962, determined not to become another painter of wee harbours and fishing boats.) The new generation of Glasgow artists have, with their aggressive approach and uncompromising painting, staged a convincing revolt against this mediocre and dull traditionalism re-establishing those links with the main currents of modern art and thought which were an essential part of all progressive Glaswegian art movements earlier in the century and in so doing properly reflect the city's current status as "the most developed, cosmopolitan metropolis in Scotland."

A door had opened! The world was as ever-changing as ever. There was a "shift from relative simplicity and conviction to growing complexity and doubt." This shift had been slow in Scotland. Scepticism and uncertainty have laid a heavy weight on Scotland, and the answer expected from artists and writers has been to escape if possible. Joan Eardley, called up during the war, typifies this delayed reaction to the bigger picture or the opening door. Her generation felt the five years of the Second World War like an enormous delay in something essential. Artists in Britain had been cut off from the world's art scene. In fact, the world's art scene disappeared and needed somebody like Picasso to reinvent it. Great gaps appeared in awareness, and one was almost encouraged to be as parochial as possible.

It had taken me until the sixties to see artists such as Alan Davie and Arshile Gorky. Last night, I had to answer the question: "How do you define your art?" I was in a BBC programme with my daughter, Gwen. Gwen recorded in New York. I was recorded in a studio in Glasgow. The Presenter, Mark Stephen, was located in Aberdeen, and the producer, Phil Syme, was in Inverness. Radio Scotland!

We were in a programme called "A Chip Off the Old Block." Gwen went first. She had been living in Brooklyn for nearly ten years and had been a full-time artist all her life. She gave a well-developed Précis of her interest in the woman's body and her intense objectivity and spiritual life within her painting. Through the door and beyond! I came next. I saw clearly in my mind my interest in human material, man and woman, their inventions, their stories told in their machines, making the invisible visible. I was writing this book, *The Naked Pilot*. As father and daughter, we were going to talk about our early start in art and the advantages and disadvantages of taking up the same profession.

I sat in a tiny room, alone with my microphone and headphones. It was just like an aeroplane cockpit. The programme took off, cruised, and landed. Gwen gave a great picture of Fetternear, this old school and schoolhouse in Aberdeenshire that had such an influence on her and the whole family. "We were like four islands floating alongside each other," she said. There's no doubt that, to the Hardie family, Fetternear was the heart of the matter, the space to think and develop. It provided a space to focus on painting and pottery or even rebuilding old motorcycles and cars. I exercised my eyes by focusing on a book and then refocusing as quickly as possible on the distant hills and then moving back to the printed page. Fetternear was a kind of nursery for all the family members and all our dreams. We shouldn't have left, but we did. And we were going to open doors, all right. Question: "How did you get started?"

It's always an interesting question. I have to go back to Larkhall Academy. Back to my art teacher, Jim Barclay. Here was an art teacher who kept his work in the art room. He was always carving away at his sculpture or working on school projects. He taught painting by saying he was a sculptor, but his fiancée, Margaret Horner, was a post-diploma painter still in the Art School in Glasgow. He explained tone and colour and texture and composition. And those four ideas still seemed like fresh fields to Jim Barclay, the sculptor. Somehow, he used those ideas to communicate effectively the trial-and-error side of trying to paint.

Jim talked about Glasgow School of Art, which I had only seen standing outside in Renfrew Street. Enthusiastically, he told me to go to Saturday morning classes at the art school, and he drew a wonderful map of the route from Central Station, Glasgow out onto Gordon Street, then right up Hope Street. From there, I was instructed to turn right on up the hill of Hope Street to the famous Sauchiehall Street before turning up to Renfrew Street. He said I would know when to turn up to Renfrew Street because I'd see the McLellan Galleries and Trerons & Cie. And with another turn, I'd see the GSA. His map was drawn with all the verve of a post-diploma sculptor who had hoped for a job in the sculpture department of the art school. Another sculpture post-diploma student had got that job, and poor Jim had arrived in Larkhall Academy instead.

I wish I had kept his map. It was like an open door to a new world. The actual class on a Saturday morning consisted of ten sessions of plaster cast drawing. No explanations, no tone, colour, etc., just some mumbled acknowledgement not to shade the dirt on the sculptures, but to try to remember that the upper planes were the lightest and the side planes were a bit darker. So typical of Glasgow School of Art, where the dullest ideas sat beside the sparks of excitement that come from the odd gifted student and tutor.

I did meet some of the young men and women who would form the 1955 full-time diploma course and got used to the strange McIntosh building that was to be so familiar and unfamiliar for the years ahead. The Charles Rennie McIntosh building was so different compared to any other building I had ever seen.

The public buildings in Scotland usually looked like Greek temples on the outside and nothing much on the inside. Here was an architect who thought differently and actually put that thought into practice. I think this must have been the first time I had ever come across international art in post-war Scotland. Not that we art students appreciated the dark, draughty, unusual building. We scarcely knew where to sit. Here were booths outside the huge studios where thirty-four students could sit and discuss, smoke, or gossip. But our culture criticised all this. We needed wild, Bohemians such as Alan Fletcher, Carol Gibbons, and Alasdair Gray to educate us and turn us into art students. It took time.

Amy, my elder daughter, made a film, *The Edge of Dreaming,* that questions storytelling and makes a number of connections between living and dying. *Story* is from the Welsh root *to see,* and to see was the heart of the matter in an art school education. I started well with Jim Barclay and Larkhall Academy, but it was difficult to hold on to my story amid the distractions of the art school. I'd loved getting away from the art school for my summer jobs, and the feeling of freedom I got from the city and its famous fogs of the fifties. When I returned as a tutor in 1980, I found there had grown a nucleus of talented and courageous art students who wanted to tell stories against all the fashion of contemporary art. They succeeded brilliantly. Established artists thought it was a fairy tale, a fantasy, an impossible task.

John Bellany, a Scottish contemporary painter born Port Seaton and George Basilitz, a German contemporary painter added their views to the first German art exhibition in Britain in 1986. There were storytellers with stories that pulled no punches and were uncompromising. These stories were ambitious, but more importantly, they tried to deal with the neurosis of the twentieth century that was in its final years. This was the scene for the next fifteen years. GSA retrieved its reputation as a European art school, and like the French Revolution, it was heaven to be alive.

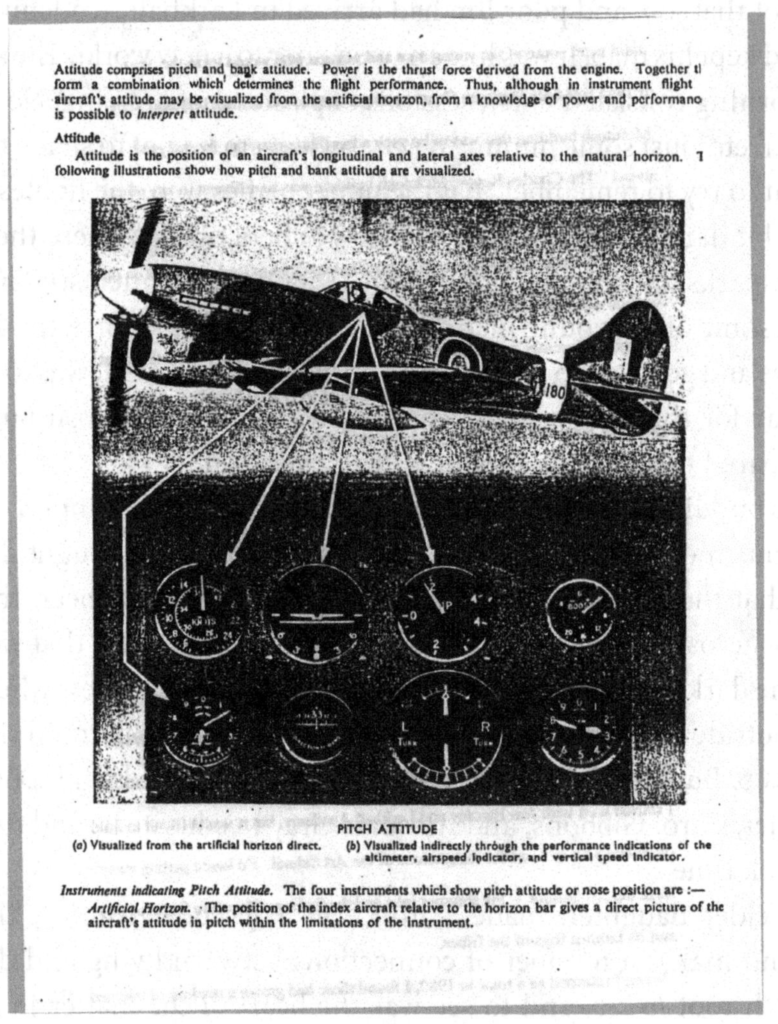

Attitude comprises pitch and bank attitude. Power is the thrust force derived from the engine. Together tl form a combination which determines the flight performance. Thus, although in instrument flight aircraft's attitude may be visualized from the artificial horizon, from a knowledge of power and performano is possible to *interpret* attitude.

Attitude

Attitude is the position of an aircraft's longitudinal and lateral axes relative to the natural horizon. 1 following illustrations show how pitch and bank attitude are visualized.

PITCH ATTITUDE

(*a*) Visualized from the artificial horizon direct. (*b*) Visualized indirectly through the performance indications of the altimeter, airspeed indicator, and vertical speed indicator.

Instruments indicating Pitch Attitude. The four instruments which show pitch attitude or nose position are :—

Artificial Horizon. The position of the index aircraft relative to the horizon bar gives a direct picture of the aircraft's attitude in pitch within the limitations of the instrument.

Pitch Attitude, 2009

I studied a bit more flying, too. By 1980, Peter Forbes's flying lessons were beginning to dim. I decided to take an Instrument Meteorological Conditions (IMC) rating. I then met two old flying instructors at Prestwick Flight Centre, Tony Angus and Les Bolton.

Tony gave me a copy of a wonderful book, the RAF's *Attitude Flight.* He had spent a lot of the war in the Empire Test Pilots School and had flown every RAF type except the Hurricane and Spitfire. When he flew the AA5 training aeroplane, I thought the instruments were stuck because the needles didn't move at all. What an example of practised professionalism. My instrument flying was a lot different; the idea was still visual coordination. It was all down to the scan of the instruments that were arranged on the instrument panel and were scanned so that corrections could be made. By the time I had scanned the six instruments, number one was hurrying off somewhere else. It was a bit like the art school! The view from the cockpit, the view from 167 Renfrew Street, open doors and closed cockpits are a wonderful combination for art and life. The secret is to keep breathing.

The story and the narrative:- Amy had found out a lot about survival in life and survival in art in her documentary *A Beginners Guide to Dying.* She had tried all sorts of techniques to connect to her audience. She felt her film had to communicate and locate death to mortals who perhaps didn't want to know about such things. She eventually fell back on the story, a much more powerful form than she realised. Even the powerful narrative of her film was shaped by her story. She found out that narrative is derived from the Latin *gnarus* or *knowing,* and *story* comes from the Welsh root *to see.* In oral cultures, story implied guidance, direction, instruction, and knowledge.

The storyteller was originally a seer or teacher who guided the souls of his listeners through the world of mystery, which is also this world, the angelic space between the divine and the chaotic – Blake's eternity in an hour of storytelling. The oral storyteller suspends time in the immediacy of his or her presence and in the improvised interplay of teller and audience; the story is alive, immediate, and eternal. Through developing patterns of meaning and catharsis, the listener is released from time and his or her human self. The pleasure is both aesthetic and emotional.

Is our life and work ruled by stories? We object so much if someone tells our story incorrectly. Their version of our emotional story shakes us to the core and takes us into a world where we are released from our human selves. The catharsis is such pain and anguish.

In August 1984, Stephen Campbell drew a man in tweeds flying through the air. It was his vision of the artist as a latter-day shaman, revelling in the power to order his own world, capable in his creative ecstasy of suspending even the laws of gravity. There is only one snag: his hair is on fire. Icarus will come down in flames even though he is only a few feet up. As Stephen Campbell, a Scottish contemporary painter, said, "The painting starts off as one thing, and if that doesn't work, I try something else until a memory of all these things is in it. But none of them is particularly true except the one I've picked to title the work. The picture is a summing up of all the mistakes: it's what's left."

Instrument Flying

All the instrument flying was very much with an instructor sitting in the right-hand seat of the aeroplane doing all the radio and organising all the arrangements with air traffic control. It was a bit of a shock when I tried it without the instructor.

The decisions to go or not to go are still the most trying. The weather changes so much over the United Kingdom, but it is well forecasted and just takes time to work out. My first real IMC flight was to Leeds/Bradford in Yorkshire. Quite high up in Yorkshire, the aerodrome being some 680 feet up in the hills, it felt like a "Good Day Out" with Wallace and Gromit, but without Gromit doing all the work.

The private pilot with three passengers who have rarely flown in a light aircraft has to do all the work. Good R T is essential, but all the flying, and changing the radio frequencies, navigation system, ADF, and the ILS are entirely up to the lone pilot (as well as flying accurately under the direction of the air traffic controllers). It's very different when there's another pilot in the right-hand seat.

Flying is all about preparation and visualising the flight using the current air charts, where air regulations are marked clearly with heights of hills, air corridors, and navigational aids. One draws out the flight with a black line and measures the distance with a ruler. The waypoints are filled in the kneepad flight plan there's a small slide rule computer for speed and time to fly these waypoints, so it's good to sit in a quiet place and work all this out with sketch diagrams of airports and think ahead to try to visualise any confusions or problems. The more experience the pilot has, the better this visualisation will be, especially if the pilot has done the flight before or seen it all in very different weather. This sense of form of the flight is quite like drawing a kind of 3D drawing in the sky.

I think, *Will we be above the cloud or underneath it? If we go above the cloud, can we get back below safely?* I remember Amy Johnson's words: "I'll just go over the top of the weather." It's a wonderful place to be, above the carpet of clouds and in the sunshine. It's real progress for the private pilot after trying for so long to keep in sight of the surface and out of the clouds. But where are you in relation to the ground you can't see? That's the big question.

It all depends on the instruments. For this trip in 1984, the aeroplane is fitted with King KNS 80 navigation. One can lay in waypoints using stations that are dotted around the United Kingdom. These are like a compass rose with a radio frequency, so one can tune in and measure the miles and direction. This data is entered into our instruments, and a station will show a left or right correction, and with distance measuring equipment (DME), we have an accurate position.

It's all very easy on the ground in that quiet place; it's different with the engine running and passengers asking about this and that. The workload for a solitary pilot is interesting, and distractions have to be recognised and put in their place.

Back to Prestwick on 18 July 1984:- X-ray uniform is a Grumman Tiger. I have come up in the world from the old Traveller and Cheetah and now have another 50 bhp. It's an amazing feeling to be zooming off into the clouds bound for Yorkshire. Prestwick glints in the sun, and there's gin-clear visibility to the south with lots of white clouds scattered about giving all sorts of options to fly around, through, over, or under. Wonderful!

The bigger engine wants to climb, and up through the scattered clouds we go. We settle just above the clouds and get on track for Deans Cross on the other side of the Solway Firth. Through breaks in the cloud, we see Dumfries, but gradually, we get forced higher and higher. We are now on flight levels with separation kept by flying different heights for different directions. We settle first for 5,500 ft, but we gradually come to 7,500 ft. Now there's such a thing as an air corridor, and my plan is to fly underneath it. Amber-1 is not so very far, and I must ask permission to cross, when we come to it, of course. We fly on a good hour and have not seen the ground since the Solway Firth. For Leeds/Bradford, I like to arrive at Keighley, which is a visual reporting point (VRP) for Leeds.

Just as I am thinking of making a call to London FIR, I get an unwelcome message in my earphones. "XU, you are contravening the lower height regulations for Amber 1. What are your intentions?"

I have been forced up gradually to FL 75, and some of Amber 1 has a lower level of FL 55. The top level, by the way, is FL 125 (12,500 ft). I ask politely for a transit across Amber 1 at my flight level. The sky up here is a winsome blue, totally clear, and not an aeroplane in sight for 100 miles.

The controller insists I am contravening the regulations and that he must report me. This is a lot to take in over the clouds and slipping along at 120 knots. I change course to cross the air lane, like crossing a busy road at right angles to the traffic, making the transit as quick as possible. The ATC keeps coming back to the contravention, and it certainly creates tension and distraction. He sounds very new to the job, and it's a great relief to raise Leeds and come under their control. I am going to fly under radar control and will fly completely blind right down to the downwind leg of the duty runway.

The cockpit goes quiet as we start our descent. I see the carpet of cloud coming nearer and nearer, and what a strange feeling it is to slide into this great, woolly canopy below which the familiar earth with all its details must still be breathing away.

After Amber 1, the new controller is quiet and reassuring. He asks me to repeat all his directions and notices any deviation on his radar screen. This voice is the only connection I have to home and beauty. We manoeuvre in thick, dark clouds, and I'm hardly able to see the wingtips.

Lower and lower, adjust the speed, and there it is: "Now look up, you're on the downwind leg for runway 14." Wow, so I am!

My partner, Pam, returns from her trade fair in Harrogate as evening sets in. After the flight down from Scotland, I feel much more confident and ready to use the sky like some great 3D chessboard to revel in the moves we must make. The aircraft AA5 Tiger is quite difficult to fly on instruments – quite skittish – but everything works well and with all the seats filled, off we go into the cloudy evening, boldly asking air traffic for various climbs and levels. We retrace our route from the morning flight, and with the setting sun in the west, we have a kind of golden glow even in the halls and towers of cloud. The feeling for the new IMC pilot is much more relaxed after the first flight without the instructor. Somehow, the most important part of flying is doing it oneself.

I try numerous flight levels in the glittering evening. The Tiger runs out of climbing ability around 9,000 feet, and the air is thinning not just for our internal combustion engine, but for our four pairs of lungs. What dimensions the sky has.

As I climb away from Yorkshire over the Lake District, I pass through a layer of scattered clouds and behold there is a magnificent hot air balloon flying at about 4,000 ft. I wonder whether he's going to fly across Amber 1 and give a wave. I ask ATC about balloons, but they tell me confidently that none are reported in my vicinity. Perhaps they don't show up on the radar.

Bye, bye, Vincenzo Lunardi. One day your balloon will fly its path again – though it might take a few years. Later that summer, I receive a visit from the Civil Aviation Authority in respect of my contravention of Amber-1!

The inspector asks me to meet him in a place of my choosing. I choose the Glasgow School of Art. How interesting to be told off in this old building among all the art students for drawing the wrong line somewhere in the sky. The inspector is sympathetic, calm, and persistent. He shows me a transcript of my radio telephone. This is very humbling as it's full of *ohs* and *ahs* – hesitations and a determination not to be distracted by anybody over the clouds! He certainly gets his point across. When I ask what the answer would be, he told me that a 180-degree turn round and back to Prestwick would be the official solution. It reminds me of that flight up in Aberdeenshire when I had to do a 180-degree turn back to the Ythan all those years ago. He does say that there is fault on both sides: the AT controller hadn't been very helpful, and there was something to be learned on both sides.

We were sitting in the refectory of the art school. When waiting for the CAA man to show up, I had mentioned to some art students that I was being investigated not by the *polis,* but by the CAA. I realised that the CAA sounds very like the CIA, and these art students were keeping their eyes on me. In the quietist moment, when he was showing me the transcripts of my faltering radio conversation, when my face had its most guilty look, a nearby pool player just about landed his pool ball in our laps! *Was it a sign from above or an Indiana Jones-style distraction,* I wondered. I thanked the inspector and returned to my studio in the hen-run of the McIntosh building, still carrying a line in the sky to my next painting. (A year later, the lower boundary of Amber I was raised to FL 7,500.)

Vincenzo Lunardi

Is Vincenzo Lunardi's toast – "Lunardi, the favourite of the ladies – more of a key to his efforts than I first realised? Do women "adore the bold"?

Chris Lee has been talking to Real Artists Partnerships and is working on the script for *First Flight in Scotland 1785.* He's interested in the elements: air, water, fire, and earth. He sees men challenging women over these elements, wanting to be gods (not mere mortals in abeyance to the beauty of women).

Hydrogen, air, fire, earth, and water play such a part of our story that our film should take an imaginative dynamic to really transcend the earth. Chris wants to work the elements, and the door has to be opened. Do we bring Icarus and Pegasus into our elemental image? Can we tell a story that creates a bigger picture? Can we touch "the mighty breath" that sweeps through Lunardi?

Is there a bargain to be struck with the gods? The Greeks seemed to see such a big picture: fate, catharsis, vanity, and contrition. At last, my old aeroplane is ready for a test. The hydraulic pressure is restored. With green lights very difficult to see, I ask Adnan to confirm their existence, and he does. I am allowed only two circuits of Prestwick. The wind is 250/10 knots. Just right for 21/3, but this runway is closed and will not be opened even for a vintage permit to fly.

My altimeter is wonky. When I set the morning's pressure, the altimeter should show 60 ft, but mine shows 1,600 ft.

Number two magneto has a drop of at least 100 revs. To go or not to go, that is the question. I rev the engine up and lean the mixture. There's an improvement, but not much. We go. Keep your eye on me, Wilbur. *Am I a Wilbur or an Antaeus?*

Antaeus, the Greek god who got his strength from the earth seems a part of "clinging to the planet as if they would grow roots." Hercules lifted him up into the air and crushed him in a wrestling match. The German painter, Georg Basilitz, used this symbol in his painting and work, which had a big influence on Scottish painting, especially in the Glasgow School of Art.

After my test-flight round the circuit of Prestwick, I find myself motorcycling the next day to Inveraray in Argyll. I cross the ferry and smell the sea. May seems so fresh, and the elements seem so friendly in the sunshine. The warmth of the sun seems to affect machinery, including aeroplanes and motorcycles. The Icarus side and the Antaeus side are easier to see, and the sense of air and ozone feels good to the airman and the earthman. We describe the air and earth by our real movement through them, which gives us our imaginative dialogue. Our connections are potent. Our fellow humans are all trying to make their own connections. We watch each other like some great queue at a traffic stop. My aches and pains seem to disappear in the sun as I register the elements in our here-and-then century.

I read a wonderful article on the history of these matters. J. G. Ballard is reviewing a book, *The Spectacle of Flight: Aviation and the Western Imagination 1920–1950* by Robert Wohl: [11] "Even flying feels all too twentieth century though millions of us take to the air as casually as we board a bus or train. We wait in nondescript boarding lounges, walk down metal tunnels, and lever ourselves into the narrow seats of a small cinema, where we watch Hollywood films on a low-definition screen while unsmiling staff push trays onto our laps bearing an assortment of inedible foods that we are not expected to eat.

"Before takeoff, the cabin crew perform a strange folkloric rite that involves synchronised arm movements and warnings of fire and our possible immersion in water, all presumably part of an appeasement ritual whose origins are back in the prehistory of the propeller age. The ceremony, like the transubstantiation of the host, has no meaning for us, but it is kept alive by the airlines to foster a sense of tradition. After a few hours, we leave the cinema and make our way through another steel tunnel into an identical airport in the suburb of a more or less identical city. We may have flown thousands of miles, but none of us has seen the outside of the aircraft and could not even say if it had two, three, or four engines. All this is called air travel.

"The miracle and wonder of flight, which has inspired poets and philosophers and madmen, has dwindled into a workaday procedure that we anticipate with the same enthusiasm we feel when we visit the dentist. Faced with the monotony and sheer hard work of being an airline passenger, it's unbelievable that only a few decades ago, flying enthralled everyone on our planet, kindling hopes of a happier and closer world.

"The aeroplane soon became the main exemplar of a modernist aesthetic, praised by architects for its heroic purity of line and function, an appeal that wasn't lost on the fascist dictators of the day. Mussolini believed that a new civilisation would be created by aviation, fusing advanced machines with the steely-eyed heroes who controlled them.

"Reading the passionate claims made by the poet and fascist ideologue Gabriele D'Annunzio and the sense of the sacred invoked by the mail pilot and novelist Antoine de Saint-Exupéry, it's easy to forget that the gilded chariots described in their overheated rhetoric were flimsy structures of wire, spruce, and painted canvas with little more than lawnmower engines to carry them over mountain ranges and deserted oceans.

"The feats involved flying without rescue ships or radio navigation were clearly heroic and the general public after the First World War desperately needed heroes. Aviation, the writer Robert Wohl comments, attracted people who sought strong emotion and intense experience and were prepared to pay for them with short lives.

"The pilot, magician, and raconteur, Saint Exupéry, was a complex but attractive figure. The great poet of the sky, the author of *Night Flight* and the children's classic, *The Little Prince,* the man wrote mystically about the solitude of the cockpit, the wonder of clouds and airborne time, the terror of storms, and the pilot's inevitable desire for death. A tall, shambling figure, he was unhappily married and the most romantic hero that aviation has yet produced, dying at the controls of his Lightning fighter when he was shot down into the sea near Toulon in 1944.

"Aviation, like powerboating, has always been a rich man's sport, and record-breaking flights in the pre-war years were financed like independent film productions with money desperately scrounged from the press and publicity-hungry politicians. Like independent film, it attracted a great many mavericks, including a few incompetent pilots who today would never be allowed into the air. Indeed, there are those who think that Saint-Exupéry was one of them. But there was no aviation bureaucracy to stifle initiative and smother the life from our most wild and impractical dreams. Aviation was then so new there were few social or career restraints and a large number of woman pilots carried out record-breaking flights and become even greater stars than most of their male rivals. Amelia Earhart who vanished in the Pacific; Amy Johnson who plunged into the Thames Estuary during the war; Beryl Markham who gave her own private spin on the notion of the erotic cathexis of flight.

"There were a host of others, usually photographed in white overalls leaning against their flying machines. Flight and beauty fused, and it's hard to believe that any of these remarkable women would die. Sadly, dozens of them did while setting off across huge distances with little more than a compass, a packet of sandwiches, and a plucky smile."

What would Vincenzo Lunardi think of all this, 165 years after his landing in Fife? Vincenzo took his cat and his pigeon into the air and kept in touch somehow with both Icarus and Antaeus. Here's to Pitscottie on 5 October 1785!

Test Pilot

I join the Light Aircraft Association (LAA) to try to keep costs down. Engine rebuilds are more expensive than rebuilding your life, so when the time comes for the annual permit to fly renewal, I try it the LAA way.

As the owner of GBSMD, I can apply to be recognised as the test pilot for the Nord 1101 and duly get a certificate to this effect. Pilots recognised for testing this aeroplane: Hugh Copeland and Jim Hardie. The schedule for the test is four pages long with all sorts of data and manoeuvres. The big difference is the weight. Full fuel, about fifty-five gallons and three hundred pounds in the back seat of the four seat aeroplane. Where the VIPs used to sit, we now heft six weights, each fifty pounds, each equivalent to two rear passengers (or one fat Luftwaffe general).

We use the safety belts and elastic cords to secure the weights. The seats in the back will never be the same. The poor aeroplane sits down a bit at the tail, but it copes well with its designed load. We have to do three stalls, and we don't want fifty-pound weights coming through the cockpit windscreen.

The most interesting items in the flight test schedule are the climb, dive, and stall. But even getting the Nord through its ground checks takes time. We have a Mag-Drop on number two Magneto, which turns out to be the famous number five cylinder spark plug. The end of the HT lead must have been fried during the engine failure of last year and needs sorting.

After two attempts, we manage to get off the ground and into the aerial world on a Sunday afternoon of high cloud and warm, windy air. George McNaughton comes along as observer and fills in the schedule. We start the climb near the Heads of Ayr. 83 Knots is the best rate of climb, and we set this on our air speed indicator with full power and the ball in the middle at all times.

There's a wonderful message through the stick and rudder bars as the streamlined, old aeroplane with undercarriage up and propeller in automatic sits in its effective position and climbs majestically up the sky for five minutes on George's stopwatch. Never mind the money never mind the false starts, the machine is in its element even after sixty-two years of flying.

I concentrate on the stalls. *With all this weight in the back of the aeroplane, will the stall be affected?* I wonder. The first stall is in clean configuration (undercarriage up and flaps up). Ball in the middle, ease back the throttle, and pull the stick gently. Under 50 knots, there is a slight buffeting and flight is restored by releasing the pressure on the stick and increasing the power. This is done at a height of 3,500 ft … just in case we have a wing drop.

The next stall is in take-off configuration (flaps down, 15, and undercarriage down). This time, the speed drops to 38 knots before the buffet and is amazingly stable, which gives me and George a bit more confidence. The third stall is the important one (the aeroplane dressed up for landing, flaps down, 40, undercarriage down). Again, a very gentle buffet and no difference between fully laden and part laden. Under 38 knots, the indicator is up against the stop. What an amazing, old aeroplane she is. As the nose drops and the power is eased on and off, we fly for another sixty-two years!

Dancer On A Wing, 2009

All that holds an aeroplane in
the air, whether Jumbo Jet or a
sixty-two-year-old Nord is the air
passing over the wings. The upper
skin is shaped in a curve, and the
lower skin is nearly flat. That's it.

The speed of the air creates lift on these surfaces, but only at certain angles. When the angle gets too great or the speed of the air gets too slow, the wing loses its lift. It's all very straightforward, but it's a lesson that must never be ignored!

Next comes the dive to Vne (velocity never exceeds). The schedule says, "Increase speed up to Vne at shallowest dive angle possible by maintaining sufficient power but keeping RPM within maximum permissible. If any unusual airframe or control vibration is felt, immediately reduce speed by closing the throttle and gradually pulling the control column back. Record."

The afternoon sky is smooth and empty, and the old aircraft takes the speed smoothly – credit to old Willie Messerschmitt and the French designers. A classic is always a classic. The testing time goes on and on. The whole summer of 2009 seems to enter a limbo as delays and false starts hold the flying to hardly an hour or two. Making the film, *The First Flight in Scotland,* is the priority, but sadly, the weather breaks and autumn gives its misty, wet atmosphere to our ideas.

The Dream of Flight

Prestwick Airport, Saturday 26 September 2009

I'm lying on my back under a very oily aeroplane. The streaks of oil seem like telltales for the passing airstream. I clean the oil off the landing light using petrol from the fuel tap under the fuselage. It always amazes me that the glass over the camera is so clean. I wipe and wipe, and then I climb out from under the plane up to the cockpit and clean the windscreen above the second camera. The two Bullet cameras are fed to camcorders, and my assistant Tamara Polajnar, tests them with a lapful of wires, leads, batteries, and blinking lights.

Saturday promises sunshine in the east but rain and clouds in the west. I wonder where the changeover of the weather will occur – halfway or nearer Edinburgh and Fife. Tamara and I install ourselves in our classic. We've emptied the aeroplane of unnecessary weight because we want to experiment with steep turns and manoeuvres to bring into play our two cameras.

The propeller is in fine pitch, and we get the engine started and switch on the radio. There's a snag because the compressor knob doesn't turn to build up the pressure for restarting. The engine has a lack of compression on two cylinders and barely makes 2,000 revs on the ground run. The propeller pitch just doesn't work; it seems to be stuck in fully fine, which is what we need for take-off, landing, and the manoeuvres for our photography.

We depart runway 31 with a right turn out for Kilmarnock and the Garnock Valley. All these motorcycle runs on my classic motorbike give me a clear picture of the ground I am now flying over. Louden Hill sits like a shapely carbuncle up the Garnock valley. I've got two flight plans. If the cloud base is too low, I can fly from Strathhaven to Larkhall and right across to Edinburgh, entering the zone at Polmont. If the cloud base allows, I can fly from Strathhaven to Lanark and south of the Pentlands to Penicuik and come round to Edinburgh by Arthurs Seat and Leith Harbour.

We're trying to catch the evening light when the shadows are long to create a sculptured feel to the ground, which brings out the sense of the features we still have in common with the eighteenth-century Lunardi flight some 224 years ago!

The clouds are low and ragged, but it's possible to break through, and there's a terrific change as we fly over the hills to Penicuik. There's Tinto Hill – unmistakable with its cairn at the top of its smooth, rounded shape. Again, I am reminded of the motorbike runs. The light increases and the rain stops. There's also plenty of sun. As the sun gets lower and we fly to the east following its rays, we can see intricate detail, but only in the west-east direction.

We fly past Lanark Loch and set a heading of 70 degrees magnetic into the hills. There's the Pentlands, and we can line up with their west-east position. We fly right over my daughter's farm near West Linton, and I can see right into her farmyard.

I ask Edinburgh for entry into their control zone at Penicuik and request flight over Arthur's Seat to Leith. The radio's not so strong at this height and with these hills, but the light on Edinburgh and the Firth of Forth is wonderful. We're in luck at last.

The sense of Lunardi and his first flight comes back to us as we're held over Leith by the ATC. Airliners are approaching up the Firth of Forth, and we are not allowed to fly across their descent. So we hold Leith Harbour and fly slowly in circles. As we turn into the low sun, all the detail disappears and submerges in the haze of September light.

Lunardi flew his balloon in the autumn of 1785, and he probably saw similar light. We circle for ages round and round the chessboard of Leith and the sea.

We cross the Firth of Forth behind the traffic and sway gently over Inchkeith and on to Kirkcaldy. I plan to balloon along the coast, swaying from the land to the sea until, at Lower Largo, we can line up Largo Law and fly due north.

We are now in brilliant visibility, and Ceres is clear ahead. Look east from Ceres, and there is the road from Pitscottie that goes round the landing ground of 1785, North Calange. I notice the mustard-coloured farmhouse that looked on to the memorial slab of Vincenzo Lunardi's flight of 1785.

Born in Lucca, Italy in 1759, he ascended in a hydrogen balloon on 5 October 1785 from the Garden of Heriot's Hospital, Edinburgh. He landed at Coaltown of Calange in the parish of Ceres after having travelled 46 ml. This was the first aerial voyage in Scotland. Later that month, he tried again and crashed into the sea off the Isle of May. He and his balloon were picked up by a fisherman.

The Firth looks empty this Saturday evening. There are no small boats, and the fishing boats all seem to go farther afield these days, so we head out over Anstruther, out to the May. The low light seems to eat into the cliffs and rocks of the island. The lighthouse is probably not manned, and the sculptured shapes are bathed in the light-ochre glow of the September sun, which gives the May a strange, uniform wash of colour.

We circle round and round, wondering whether Lunardi thought this was far enough and decided to let down before he was blown over the North Sea. The waves look rough and beautiful and wonderfully dark as we turn up towards the west. Our windscreen now catches the light, and our visibility disappears directly ahead in the direction of Prestwick.

I don't feel I have done justice to Lunardi's flight. The visuals seem so ordinary; I'm still looking for a powerful image, and I find it in the Bass Rock. As we fly from the Isle of May to Berwick Law, we pass the Bass.

Here is a mysterious image at last for *The Dream of Flight.* The dark, near-purple shadow of the Bass Rock stretches away down the Firth of Forth, and the massive rock has a strange patina of almost luminous purple on top. It's thousands and thousands of sea birds moulding themselves to this massive sculpture. As the birds fly off the rock, they become white against the dark, shadowy sea. The surfaces of the Bass are unlike anything I've ever seen and give me the image of a kind of atomic reactor pulsing away in the sunlight and throwing off atoms in an almost haphazard way

We leave the Bass with reluctance to head back to the Lothian coast. Now we're heading directly into the sun instead of lighting, and it seems to stop our vision at the very windscreen of the aeroplane.

We can still see clearly to the side, but not directly ahead. Our view is now the marks and blotches of an old Perspex windscreen. I steer 240 M and align myself with the Pentland Hills, this time going the opposite way. When you can't see very well ahead, it's difficult to compare one place to another directly ahead – they're only clear as you pass them. *So is that town Penicuik, or is it that town down there?* I wonder.

Luckily, I am exactly on the track of my outward journey. There again is Amy's farm, only this time a light aircraft turns up on my nose from an airstrip only a few hundred yards from the farm. I turn away as the microlight aircraft turns the opposite way and disappears into the light. Flying seems to bring out these apparitions, these motes in the eye and these strange marks on the windscreen as the low light dictates what we try to recognise as something familiar.

From Lanark and the River Clyde, I can see some 20 mi to Louden Hill, again with its characteristic silhouette clear against the light. This makes it simple to rejoin Prestwick control zone at Kilmarnock and head back for an evening landing on runway 21 with the wind at 240/12 knots. I can't wait to see the three hours of MiniDV tape on Vincent Lunardi's epic flight in his balloon on 5 October 1785.

Don't Let the Monsters Eat Your Heroes

This Friday, I'm taking one and a half hours away from the earth. I'm taking a time capsule over Lanarkshire and disconnecting my connections. Humanity is left somewhere below, and the naked pilots are somewhere in the ether.

I remember reading a book about shark attacks, *Close to Shore*, by Michael Capuzzo. Puny humans swimming along the beach were attacked and eaten by a monster. This is very unusual despite all the stories. And the reason it's so unusual is that humanity doesn't like letting go of even one puny swimmer. In 1916, the swimmers who were attacked on the New Jersey beaches in New York were defended by thousands who rushed to their rescue. It's one of the strange characteristics of the human race: we're all there for one another like it or lump it. And there's a lot more of us than any other species. There's something of this in the disappearances of pilots: a sense that it's impossible to let go of Amelia Earhart, Saint-Exupéry and Amy Johnson. They're out there being attacked by monsters.

Even in the case of the most blissful flying weather with perfect visibility and no wind or bumps over the hills, there's a sense of déjà vu as you fly over your home village changed so much in the last seventy years. But there's Machanhill Primary School, Larkhall, and its low buildings are still the same colour. There's Union Street Primary School with its school meals building next to it where we saw films to the background smell of cabbage and mince. One can only disconnect for seconds; connections roll in like stories and lines of poems that were learned by rote.

I fly round like I was visiting people a long gone. I see my brother's car isn't in his car porch. He did say he had something to do. I can hardly see 32 Glen Avenue, where I was brought up. I jiggle my wings and make a course connection like the old Vickers Viscount of the fifties. I looked up then as I look down now. I remember the sensation of being earthbound, but I didn't know the sensation of being up in the air. The aeroplane's engine is the basic difference. The propeller glitters in the sun and the pistons zip up and down to turn the crankshaft. I'm trying to find a smoother setting for the rebuilt engine, though the pitch setting does help the slight unevenness of the vibration. In the fifties, the internal combustion engines I knew were all in motorcycles.

Singles, twins, V twins, flat twins – all that clever engineering to help us out of this Clyde valley to pastures new. The fun of riding my 1000 cc V twin Brough Superior to the Art School in Glasgow at the end of the valley is still held in my memory. There is the city without smoke and fog now; it is clear and brittle with the river flowing through. It's a tremendous privilege to fly such a classic aeroplane with its connections to the thirties and forties.

The dimension of disappearance seems to need some kind of closure, no matter how absurd. There are constantly revelations years later as we fight the monsters that ate our heroes. "I shot down Amy Johnson"; "I found Saint-Exupéry's wrist chain"; "I saw Amelia Earhart"; "I saw Bill Burns' headless body." We love explanations in our own dimensions of understanding. They're so irresistible; our imagination will not be stymied.

The two wartime disappearances of Amy Johnson and Saint-Exupéry are confused in the fog of war, so many were busy disappearing alongside our two heroes. The Second World War was good at this. Was Amy Johnson on a secret mission? What was the strange floating object? Her would-be rescuer, Lieutenant Commander Fletcher died trying to rescue her in 1941. As late as 1999, a man named Tom Mitchell claimed to have shot Amy down when she gave the wrong colour of the day. After sixteen shells, a plane dived into the Thames Estuary. Was this antiaircraft fire? Sixteen shells doesn't sound like fire from an aircraft. The strange, hazy weather must have meant there was little real sighting of anything on that January day in 1941. Amy couldn't be rescued from the monster of war.

A very similar thing happened to the famous Saint-Exupéry. The French Magazine *ICARE,* which covers French Aviation, goes into Saint-Exupéry's disappearance in great detail by publishing present-day newspaper reports and essays from all who knew or met him in his last days of flying photoreconnaissance missions from the Isle of Corsica in 1944.

Even so, the mystery remains. The stories are all plausible, and at least two Luftwaffe pilots shot down Lockheed Lightning's P38 F5B. *ICARE* favours the story of Luftwaffe pilot Robert Helchele based on one letter sent to a fellow Luftwaffe pilot, Wilhelm Manz. It always sounds so reasonable and likely. The monster never has a shark's face. Like everybody else, pilots have friends and enemies who are desperate to interpret the disappearance according to their affection or antagonism.

Bill Burns, who disappeared on 14 October 1972, is the classic example. This Glaswegian lost his mother when he was 8 years old, and this had a curious effect on him. He could identify with children up to the age of 8, but his image for children ended at this magic number. After 8 years old, there was a strange, competitive aggression that crept in. Burns, as he got older, got more complicated. He became the embodiment of

Dr Jekyll and Mr Hyde – he stalked, manipulated, and bullied close to the shore. He looked like Van Dyke with a kind of mercurial intensity, just as Jimmy Scotland, the principal, described him in his obituary.

As an able man who was intelligent and imaginative, he was hamstrung by his complexes. Like Saint-Exupéry, Bill was a wonderful storyteller and saw his own life as stories rather than connections. Stories were told to suit whoever was listening, and the facts hardly came into the images he saw with such energy. Red-red, red-orange, orange … the colours were applied with such strict devotion that if the premixed colour ran out, he would scrape the area off with his palette knife and start again. He never married, and I think he had problems related to friendships and relationships.

Aberdeen College of Education, from the fifties to the seventies, had a very creative staff who appreciated Bill as the latest thing in art education, and he certainly managed to get the head job in art by any means fair or foul. Many people shunned him as a bully, but many more found him colourful, exciting, and unusual in Scottish education during this period. Do these driven characters make good teachers?

Once Bill was caught up in his self-righteousness, he could make a student go home and change into a suit for a very important student critique lesson. The student, whose sense of connection was completely broken, managed to stagger through his lesson, but something essential was lost forever. His interest in people's lives could be disastrous, and he went to all sorts of lengths to put them off marriage and childbirth. A red madness descended, and we called him the Red Baron. He left his teaching post in 1971. He must have recognised his own strange behaviour and told everybody he didn't want to live beyond 50 years of age. He implied some ancient pilot/ancient mariner ritual. So his strange accident on 14 October 1972 was well endorsed with these feelings of exhaustion, isolation, and mixed up thinking.

When flying low in mist or haar near the coast, it is not impossible to save oneself. Ball in the middle, select climbing speed by raising the nose, full throttle and climb to 2,000 feet, and try to follow the coast to where you started from. The water is on one side and the land is on the other. Fly gently straight, level, and sing a wee song.

Nearly all the pilots in the north-east of Scotland have had to do this from time to time. The trick is not to get too low in the first place.

Like Don Quixote, the monsters are all in our own heads. The naked pilots, the Jean Brodies and the Bill Burnses have a strange, demented innocence like the pilots of the Second World War. They think, "It'll never happen to me," despite evidence to the contrary.

It's very difficult to find out what really happened. So many of Bill's art students were very antagonistic towards Bill Burns. The most lurid tale I heard was that his body was washed up on the Black Dog range north of Aberdeen, some 30 mi from his crash.

An ex-student gave the image that the police took some criminal down to the morgue and showed them his headless body to frighten them into confessing to a crime.

I remember being on a beach in October 1972, looking out to sea, and remembering The Red Baron. I could only remember Mr Jekyll – his talent, ability, and wit. The sea claimed all three of my naked pilots, and it somehow seems like a restless resting place for the great innocence they shared.

Bibliography

1.Excerpt	Storytelling and Film	Brian Dunnigan
2.Excerpt	Stephen Campbell	Stuart Morgan, 1984
3.Excerpt	A Beginner's Guide to Dying	Amy Hardie, 2009
4. Excerpt	New Image Glasgow	Sandy Moffat, 1985
5.Excerpt	That Summer	Andrew Greig, 2000
6.Excerpt	First Flight	John Evangelist Walsh, 1975
7. Excerpt	Antoine de Saint-Exupéry	Curtis Cate, 1970
8.Excerpt	A Cinder Glows	Mary Morton, 1989
9. Excerpt	Education In The North	1966
10.Excerpt	Imagery, *The Source In Aesthetic Education*	William Burns, 1966
11.Excerpt	Spectacle of Flight	Robert Wohl, 2005
12. Excerpt	Strong Words	W.N. Herbert and Mathew Hollis 2000
13. Excerpt	Poems *are authors except stated otherwise*	Jim Hardie
14. Excerpt	Letters *of Rudolf Hess to his wife*	Rudolf Hess